Modern Language Association of America

Approaches to Teaching World Literature

Joseph Gibaldi, Series Editor

26. Robin Riley Fast and Christine Mack Gordon, eds. *Approaches to Teaching Dickinson's Poetry*. 1989.

27. Spencer Hall, ed. *Approaches to Teaching Shelley's Poetry*. 1990.

28. Sidney Gottlieb, ed. *Approaches to Teaching the Metaphysical Poets*. 1990.

29. Richard K. Emmerson, ed. *Approaches to Teaching Medieval English Drama*. 1990.

30. Kathleen Blake, ed. *Approaches to Teaching Eliot's* Middlemarch. 1990.

31. María Elena de Valdés and Mario J. Valdés, eds. *Approaches to Teaching García Márquez's* One Hundred Years of Solitude. 1990.

32. Donald D. Kummings, ed. *Approaches to Teaching Whitman's* Leaves of Grass. 1990.

33. Stephen C. Behrendt, ed. *Approaches to Teaching Shelley's* Frankenstein. 1990.

Approaches to Teaching Homer's
Iliad and *Odyssey*

Edited by

Kostas Myrsiades

The Modern Language Association of America
New York   1987

Library of Congress Cataloging-in-Publication Data

Approaches to teaching Homer's Iliad and Odyssey.

  (Approaches to teaching world literature ; 13)
  Bibliography: p.
  Includes index.
  1. Homer—Study and teaching. 2. Homer. Iliad.
3. Homer. Odyssey. 4. Epic poetry, Greek—
Study and teaching. I. Myrsiades, Kostas.
II. Modern Language Association of America.
III. Series.
PA4037.A5A68   1987   883'.01   86-31167
ISBN 0-87352-499-3
ISBN 0-87352-500-0 (pbk.)

Cover illustration of the paperback edition: "How Ulisses escap'd the Syrens," engraving by Peter Fourdrinier, illustration of book 12, *The* Odyssey *of Homer*, translated by Alexander Pope, 1725.

Second printing, 1989
Third printing, 1990

Published by The Modern Language Association of America
10 Astor Place, New York, NY 10003-6981

CONTENTS

PREFACE TO THE SERIES

In *The Art of Teaching* Gilbert Highet wrote, "Bad teaching wastes a great deal of effort, and spoils many lives which might have been full of energy and happiness." All too many teachers have failed in their work, Highet argued, simply "because they have not thought about it." We hope that the Approaches to Teaching World Literature series, sponsored by the Modern Language Association's Committee on Teaching and Related Professional Activities, will not only improve the craft—as well as the art—of teaching but also encourage serious and continuing discussion of the aims and methods of teaching literature.

The principal objective of the series is to collect within each volume different points of view on teaching a specific literary work, a literary tradition, or a writer widely taught at the undergraduate level. The preparation of each volume begins with a wide-ranging survey of instructors, thus enabling us to include in the volume the philosophies and approaches, thoughts and methods of scores of experienced teachers. The result is a sourcebook of material, information, and ideas on teaching the subject of the volume to undergraduates.

The series is intended to serve nonspecialists as well as specialists, inexperienced as well as experienced teachers, graduate students who wish to learn effective ways of teaching as well as senior professors who wish to compare their own approaches with the approaches of colleagues in other schools. Of course, no volume in the series can ever substitute for erudition, intelligence, creativity, and sensitivity in teaching. We hope merely that each book will point readers in useful directions; at most each will offer only a first step in the long journey to successful teaching.

Joseph Gibaldi
Series Editor

PREFACE TO THE VOLUME

Homer's epics, the first great masterpieces of world literature, composed in Greek some three thousand years ago, find themselves today occupying a position in Western culture shared only by the Bible. So pervasive are Homer's tales of the Olympian gods and the Trojan heroes that most students probably have some familiarity with the Homeric myths before the completion of their secondary education. In higher education, Homer's epics are usually the first works anthologized for the general literature courses that, at present, are required of most college students throughout the country. Because Homer's influence has touched all aspects of our culture, his epics extend beyond the confines of a specific discipline and are used with equal facility in classics, English, comparative literature, history, philosophy, and social science departments. Like the Bible, Homer is so universal that at times we are hardly aware that we are reading him in translation and not in his own language.

In this volume teachers in higher education describe the various ways they use Homer in their disciplines and introduce the reader to the importance of Homer in Western culture. The essays and materials in this volume are primarily intended for those teaching on the undergraduate level, more specifically for the nonspecialist offering general literature courses in translation. It is hoped, however, that the specialist might also find value in some of the writings in this volume. The volume may be of use, as well, to those teaching in secondary schools and to those ready to embark on a teaching career and face being asked to offer units on mythology and on Homer for which they have little formal training.

Like the other books in this series, the present volume is in two parts: "Materials" and "Approaches." The discussion of pedagogical tools in the first four sections of "Materials" is based on a survey of seventy-eight teachers of Homer in colleges and universities throughout the United States and Canada; in the last section, "The Instructor's Library," the editor compiles a collection of materials to assist the generalist in teaching Homer. Part 2, which is divided into two sections—"Teaching Homer and the Homeric Epics" and "Teaching Specific Epics"—consists of seventeen essays by specialists and nonspecialists on approaches to teaching Homer in upper-division literature courses, in survey courses, in composition courses, and in disciplines other than English and classics. Individual essays are more fully described in the introduction to "Approaches." In the spellings of Greek names, I have followed the practice of Richmond Lattimore in his translations of the *Iliad* and the *Odyssey*. Some of the more familiar Greek names have been left in their latinized forms for convenience and clarity.

Because of the wide interest in the Homeric epics and their use in many disciplines, a special effort was made to solicit questionnaire responses and essays from educators in a variety of disciplines. The 78 teachers polled include 38 in English departments, 28 in classics, and eleven in comparative literature, history, philosophy, and anthropology departments. The "Approaches" essays include contributions by English instructors, classicists, comparatists, a historian, and a philosopher. The participants in the survey of Homer instructors are listed at the end of this volume.

I wish to acknowledge my indebtedness to those educators who responded to my questionnaire on Homer and whose generous and thoughtful comments make up the first part of "Materials." I am most grateful to all the scholars and teachers who consented to write for the "Approaches" section, especially those whose work had to be omitted from the final version. Of the twenty-two essays originally considered only seventeen could be used because of space and the particular demands of the series. As always, I am indebted to my wife, Linda Suny Myrsiades, who proofread this manuscript and made many valuable suggestions. I further recognize my indebtedness to the Modern Language Association in general and specifically its Committee on Teaching and Related Professional Activities, which sponsored and supervised this project. Finally, special thanks must go to Joseph Gibaldi, general editor of this series, whose specific and detailed comments made this volume possible.

KM

Part One

MATERIALS

Kostas Myrsiades

Editions and Translations

Greek Editions

According to the survey of Homer instructors, the most popular editions for teaching the epics in the original Greek are W. B. Stanford's text for the *Odyssey* and Allen Rogers Benner's text for the *Iliad*. The Homeric volumes in the Oxford Classical Texts (OCT) series (see Allen; Munro and Allen) receive frequent mention for their accuracy and convenience as reliable guides to teaching Homer in the original, irrespective of the epic being taught.

Although some commend Stanford's copious notes and "excellent commentary," others think the text "naive about oral poetry" and burdened with an "out-of-date introduction." Benner's text is praised for its introduction, selections, grammatical commentary, and glossary, in sum, for "its magnificent apparatus." The OCT series conveniently offers complete texts of both epics; in addition, one instructor comments, "I prefer the OCT because using it forces the students to face the text more directly, unfiltered through the eyes of a modern commentator, and encourages the students to free themselves in their reading (if not in their research) from dependence upon authorities."

Translations

Nearly three quarters of those polled prefer verse over prose translations of Homer's epics. Only a fifth choose prose over poetry, while the remainder have no preference. The overwhelming reason for using a verse rather than a prose translation is to keep the distinction between poetry and prose well-defined. For some, only a verse translation expresses Homer the poet, while prose translations confuse students into perceiving the epics as a kind of early novel. Moreover, those who teach the formulaic tradition of the epics find verse close to a necessity. Many also feel that verse translations are "clearer" than prose, that they impose "a simple and lofty style which is lost in prose translations," or that verse elicits "better student response." Others find that verse preserves "the power of the original"; offers a greater "sense of convention"; conveys the patterned quality of the epics; emphasizes the uncommon, elevated, and intense language of Homer; preserves the beauty of the original; and distinguishes between Homeric formulas and the modern novel. The last group finds prose too limiting and too "chatty" for Homer's poems.

Those who use prose translations do so because they find "students can handle prose better than poetry." Comments range from "prose makes the work more accessible" and "sophomores faint when confronted with a long poem" to "many of our students have reading difficulty." Nevertheless, some instructors argue that prose can render Homer more accurately "since to try to recreate the original Greek poetry in English verse destroys the original concept." For those requiring "accurate" translations, some verse renderings are too "free," as in the Fitzgerald and Logue translations of Homer.

Interestingly, few instructors alternate between verse and prose translations, depending on the type of course. In fact, most respondents believe their selection adequate for any course they teach, whether general or specialized. The remainder of the sample, largely those based in classics departments, think the course should dictate the choice of translation: upper-division courses that cover Homer's oral art or the epic tradition should always use verse, whereas lower-division literature courses that focus on plot, character, or mythology could more appropriately be taught in prose. Those who teach the epics in Greek find a literal rather than a poetic translation more helpful as an aid to the study of grammar. In general, as one instructor put it, "verse for more literary, prose for more problem-oriented courses."

The most popular translations in current use are those of Richmond Lattimore, whose name is mentioned by nearly half the respondents. Robert Fitzgerald follows in popularity; E. V. Rieu is a distant third. The remaining translators cited include Albert Cook, T. E. Shaw, A. H. Chase and W. G. Perry, W. H. D. Rouse, and George Herbert Palmer.

The Lattimore verse translation of the *Iliad*—the preferred text of more than three-fourths of the respondents—is the most widely used text in survey as well as more specialized courses on Homer. A distant second to Lattimore's text among *Iliad* translations is Fitzgerald's poetic version. Finally, a few instructors report they are more comfortable with the translations of Chase and Perry; Alexander Pope; Chapman (ed. Nicoll); and Lang, Leaf, and Myers.

Lattimore's texts, especially the *Iliad*, receive praise for their beauty, readability, accuracy, and faithfulness to the Homeric line as well as for the translations' notes and introductions. Lattimore's translations are preferred, says one instructor, because "despite minor errors and inadequacies, I feel closer to the experience of reading the poems in Greek using [his] translations." Another states, "Lattimore's translations are far better than Fitzgerald's because they preserve all the correct connotations and poetic values while Fitzgerald's become highly impressionistic." As for Lattimore's *Iliad*, even those who use another translation in their courses agree with one instructor's assessment: "Lattimore succeeds in transmitting something of the stately and ritualized formality of the Greek without sacrificing much of the plainness and directness of style characteristic of Homer."

Those seeking an English version of Homer's *Odyssey* find a wider field to choose from. Here, the majority of instructors polled prefer the Fitzgerald verse version; Lattimore's verse rendition and Rieu's prose version tie for a distant second. A few report using Cook's verse or Shaw's prose translation.

Those who prefer Fitzgerald's *Odyssey* to Lattimore's base their choice on habit and the convenience of using a text widely anthologized in such survey course texts as *The Norton Anthology of World Masterpieces* (ed. Mack). Nevertheless, instructors also find Fitzgerald's *Odyssey* fun to read. "Since I don't know Greek," one instructor writes, "I have no idea how faithful this translation is to the original, but it is a fine poem in English, with many beautiful passages." Fitzgerald's version is thought clear, graceful, colloquially direct, readable, less literal and more incisive than Lattimore's version, and above all poetic. One instructor acknowledges that "Students overwhelmingly prefer him to Lattimore, who loses them." As another states:

> Fitzgerald believes that a poem in translation should read like an English poem—iambic pentameters for heroic verse, modulated diction, phrases that are surprisingly right. To be sure, they do not capture the formulaic style of the originals, and they alter a metaphor here and there. But they are beautiful.

Those who choose to teach using Cook's verse translation rather than Fitzgerald's or Lattimore's cite Cook's "simple language and verse patterns" and his "poetically prosaic" verse. Rieu's translation is most popular among teachers who use prose rather than verse in deference to "students [who] have read little verse" and who thus find it difficult to understand and appreciate Homer. Rieu's colloquial language and "easy trivialization" is considered readily accessible: "Even inexperienced readers get quickly caught up in the excitement of this narrative." The merits of Shaw's prose translation are cited as readability and "great faithfulness to tone and nuance." In one comment, Shaw's prose is preferred to Lattimore's for its "felicitous" rendering. (See the section on translation in "The Instructor's Library" for a discussion of the scholarship devoted to Homer translation.)

Anthologies

Nearly all those polled prefer to use complete texts of the Homeric epics rather than anthologized pieces. Yet many admit that departmental policy has led them to use anthologies in required survey courses. They cite the benefits of teaching only selections from anthologies, including the ability to cover more works in a semester and the desire to control costs for student texts. A few instructors also feel that background materials included in anthologies like the Norton series are useful for introductory literature courses. Moreover, there is a decided advantage to having comparable selections of Homer, Vergil, and Dante collected in one volume.

The overwhelming majority of instructors, however, find anthologies too limiting in teaching Homer's epics. The main issue raised is the legitimacy of studying a great work of literature by looking at only fragments of it—and those fragments selected by an editor. Respondents contend that appreciating the sweep, the shape, the form, the pace, the unity, and the expansiveness of each epic, as well as understanding the period, culture, and poetry of Homer, requires access to the whole work. In instances where time limitations do prohibit teaching the entire epic, the complete text at least allows instructors the freedom of choosing their own selections in translations they prefer. Teaching from an anthology, one instructor said, "is like listening to 'Great Themes from Tchaikovsky': you can talk about this and that, as you might whistle a tune here and there, but you do not know what has been left out." Some argue that anthologies do more than merely "select too narrowly," for "the selector or abridger of the text becomes an interpreter by the very act of abridgment." As one instructor puts it, "anthologies reflect on texts. I regard nothing as optional or superfluous."

Nevertheless, many among those who strongly object to the use of anthologies, including both those teaching Homer in the original Greek and those teaching the epics in translation in general literature courses, find it necessary at times to assign parts of required epics. In such instances, the books of the *Iliad* most often mentioned as indispensable are 1, 9, 24, 16, 18, 22, 3, and 6, in that order. In the *Odyssey*, the books mentioned most often are 1–4, 6–12, and 23, with 1 and 9 heading everyone's list.

Required and Recommended Student Readings

The survey indicates that teachers of the *Iliad* and the *Odyssey* give virtually equal emphasis to three background areas: oral epic poetry, Greek mythology, and Homeric history and culture. A number of instructors, voicing the concerns of many, stress that priority should always be given to the texts themselves rather than to background material. One respondent comments, "I regard close and sensitive reading as the main issue. It is easy and a tragic mistake to substitute 'background' for a really meaningful encounter with the text." Most would agree with two instructors, the first of whom states, "I refer to them [background materials] wherever elucidation seems helpful or interesting, but my first concern is that the students be familiar with the poem itself"; the second writes, "first and foremost the poem communicates a tremendous human experience which my classes are devoted to trying to imagine." A small minority feel that background is unnecessary in teaching the Homeric epics in introductory and general courses: "I use practically no 'background material.' The poems are long and time is short. Furthermore, they stand isolated from their time and place. Better students should learn to read and appreciate them as artworks than to see them smothered in dubious scholarship." This group finds the text, if treated well, to be self-contained: "everything necessary to understanding the poem is in the poem."

Consensus on titles for background reading was hard to reach. Of those polled, about two-thirds suggest eighty-five different titles, while the others recommend no readings at all other than the epics being taught. This latter group thinks background reading material uses time better left for the epic itself, which in survey and general courses can often be read only in part. A substantial number of instructors prefer to prepare a bibliography of recommended readings and allow students to select as many as they can handle. Indeed, only half of those who encourage background reading feel it should be required.

Instructors who do recommend specific works most often mention Cedric Whitman's *Homer and the Heroic Tradition*. Other titles recommended by many instructors include Malcolm M. Willcock's *A Companion to the* Iliad; Alan Wace and Frank Stubbings's *A Companion to Homer*; Charles Rowan Beye's *The* Iliad, *the* Odyssey, *and the Epic Tradition*; the collection of essays edited by George Steiner and Robert Fagles, *Homer: A Collection of Essays*; and Charles H. Taylor's *Essays on the* Odyssey.

Since the Homeric epics are most frequently taught in survey, general, and Greek literature courses, they are usually studied in the context of the works of such authors as Vergil, Dante, and the Greek tragedians. As one respondent comments:

> Since the Homeric poems are the greatest literary influence on Vergil's poem, and Vergil's the greatest on Dante's, we have the ideal materials for the study of the development of poetic "meaning," or the conventions of Western literature. Further, since the two Homeric poems present the archetypal "comic" and "tragic" visions, or at least forms, they are a useful introduction to Greek drama.

Such comparisons seem desirable in survey courses for several reasons: they draw distinctions between oral and literary epic poetry, demonstrate the continuity of Western culture, elucidate the journey of the hero toward a higher human understanding, characterize the heroic quest as a vital theme throughout civilization, and show the consistency and variability of ideas in Greek culture.

The influence of Homer, moreover, is so all-pervasive that he is compared to and taught with a wide variety of authors. Of the Greek authors to whom Homer is compared in both survey and specialized courses, Sophocles heads the list, followed, in order of preference, by Euripides, Aeschylus, Aristophanes, and Plato. Single titles most frequently cited include Aeschylus's *Agamemnon*, or sometimes the entire *Oresteia*; Sophocles's *Oedipus Rex* and *Antigone*; Euripides's *Medea*; and Aristophanes's *Lysistrata*.

Other writers mentioned by survey respondents include, in alphabetical order, John Barth, Blake, Boccaccio, Byron, Cervantes, Chaucer, Cicero, Dante, T. S. Eliot, Epictetus, Spenser, Goethe, Fielding, Hawthorne, Joyce, Kafka, Milton, Ovid, Pound, Rabelais, Shakespeare, Tolstoy, Voltaire, Whitman, Wordsworth, and Yeats. Homer's epics are linked as well to such disparate works as Toni Morrison's *Song of Solomon*, Njal's *Saga*, and John Ford's film classic *Stagecoach*. As one instructor states, Homer allows comparison with almost any literary work because he "provides the first concepts of the rational hero, the nature of that rationality in terms of a cultural world view, and its characteristics in terms of the insight into the nature of man, his reason for being, and his response to himself and to others."

Aids to Teaching

Most instructors use their own private teaching aids, which consist largely of slides taken from art and archaeology texts and some commercial slides of Homeric sites. Some instructors use illustrations from such sources as *The Quest for Ulysses* by W. B. Stanford and J. V. Luce and *The Adventures of Ulysses* by Erich Lessing. Cedric Whitman's *Homer and the Heroic Tradition* is a frequently cited source for diagrams on the *Iliad*. Maps are also used as visual aids and once again sources vary; some maps are hand-drawn by the instructor. It should be noted that almost half of the survey participants use no audiovisual aids in teaching the Homeric epics.

Audiovisual Materials

The film most instructors mention is Ernle Bradford's *Search for Ulysses*, originally telecast by CBS and now available on 16mm film through Carousel Films. Other films used in Homer classes include *Epic and Narrative*, a three-part film distributed by Encyclopedia Britannica Film Series (1: Structure of the Epic, 2: The Return of Odysseus, and 3: The Central Themes of the *Odyssey*); *A Singer of Tales in Gary, Indiana* by the Folklore Institute at Indiana University, Bloomington; and *Iphigenia* by Michael Cacoyiannis, a 130-minute version of Euripides's play *Iphigenia at Aulis*, filmed in Greece in 1977 and available through Cinema 5. (For additional information, including relevant mailing addresses, see Works Cited, at the end of this volume.)

Other useful film titles mentioned include *L'Odissea*—a 1911, 30-minute silent film produced in Italy and directed by Francesco Bertolini and Adolfo Padovin—and *Ulysses*, a 1955, 104-minute Italian production directed by Mario Camerini and starring Kirk Douglas and Sylvana Mangano; the latter, although a poor adaptation, includes some interesting and exciting special effects (e.g., the Cyclopes episode). Of lesser interest is *Structure of the Epic: The* Odyssey, a 27-minute film narrated by Gilbert Highet, who presents the basic framework of the epic and traces the background of the Trojan War and events in Ithaka during Odysseus's absence. This film is part of the three-part film *Epic and Narrative*, in the Encyclopedia Britannica's Humanities Series. Another film in this series—*The Greek Myths*, in two parts, each 25 minutes long—was also found useful by some instructors. The first part explores myth as primitive fiction, described as history in disguise and the outgrowth of prehistoric ritual; the second explains ancient man's development of myth to explain natural, religious, and moral phenomena.

Filmstrips and slides on Homer's epics are also available. One, *Homer's Mythology: Tracing a Tradition*, is a sound filmstrip package in three parts. Part 1, "Homer's World" (81 frames, 13 min.), examines oral composition, the role of the poet in ancient Greek society, and the importance of Homer's works. Part 2, "The *Iliad*" (92 frames, 15 min.), discusses the qualities that make an epic, Homer's use of epithets, major characters, the legendary cause of the Trojan War, and the story of the wooden horse. Part 3, "The *Odyssey*" (116 frames, 18 min.), examines the structure of the poem and significant events, introduces major characters, and emphasizes the universality of the poem's themes and its influence on later art and literature. The visual material of this filmstrip consists of photographs taken throughout Greece and southern Italy, as well as artwork and sculpture dating from ancient times to the present. The score comes largely from the work of the modern Greek composer Stavros Xarhakos.

The slide set *Greek Mythology* includes scenes from Homer in a series of one hundred color slides (35mm) reproducing the works of world painters on Greek myths. The accompanying study guide details facts about the reproductions.

Several packages of audio materials are available for the instructor of the Homeric epics. The National Radio Theatre of Chicago's eight-part adaptation *The* Odyssey *of Homer* stars Irene Worth, Barry Morse and the program host Ed Asner and consists of eight, one-hour segments; episodes contain "footnotes" in which modern experts discuss Homeric art and ancient culture.

Pacifica Tape Library offers a five-tape package of cassettes by Denys Page: (1) *The Origins of Troy*, (2) *The Oral Legacy*, (3) *The Seventh City*, (4) *Forgotten Culture*, and (5) *The Other Dark Ages*. Folkways Records has placed on one record a series of recordings made by James A. Notopoulos between 1952 and 1953. With the aid of a Guggenheim Fellowship and the American Philosophical Society, the recordings were made in villages in mainland Greece, the islands, and Cyprus. Titled *Modern Greek Heroic Oral Poetry*, the record includes parts of the Akritan Oral Cycle (based on the wars fought on the frontier provinces of Pontus and of Cappadocia under the Byzantine Empire), several Klephtic ballads, and a number of historical narrative poems from Crete and Cyprus, in particular parts of the epic romance *Erotokritos*, a masterpiece of Cretan literature written by Vitzentzos Kornaros in 1645.

Recorded readings of the Homeric epics are also of interest to instructors of Homer's works. Richard Dyer-Bennet, who accompanies himself on the harp, has toured college campuses with his readings of the *Odyssey*; his recording of the Robert Fitzgerald translation appears on twenty-four separate records under a grant from the National Endowment for the Humanities. Frank F. Fowle III, who has been performing excerpts from the *Iliad* on college campuses since 1980, has recorded that epic. Further information can be obtained from Bard Productions.

Homer and Computers

The Homeric texts have now been put into electronic form and can be purchased for study and analysis in both minicomputers and microcomputers. At present, perhaps the most extensive repository for electronic texts for Greek classics is the Thesaurus Linguae Graecae (TLG) data bank, which is continuing to expand. The American Philological Association (APA) also has Homer as well as other Latin and Greek classics in electronic form. In considering such texts, instructors should investigate the preferred tape formats their school installations can read, and they should send those specifications along with their orders to either TLG or APA. Once the electronic texts are received, they can be prepared to work on a personal microcomputer (e.g., Kermit or YTerm). Inquiries for the Homeric texts from TLG should be addressed to Theodore F. Brunner, Director, Thesaurus Linguae Graecae, Univ. of California, Irvine, CA 92717.

The electronic Homeric texts can be studied on the Ibycus System minicomputer configuration created by David W. Packard. This system operates on Hewlett-Packard hardware with an H-P 1000 series processor and the 2640 text-editing terminals. The system software includes rapid search and sort capabilities as well as a powerful text editor and formatter. For outputting purposes, the Ibycus System is able to drive a number of different printing devices, from simple matrix and fixed-type printers to sophisticated typesetting equipment; it is widely used for publication purposes. John Abercrombie of the University of Pennsylvania's Septuagint Tools Project has modified some of these software programs to work in Basic on the IBM-PC and a number of other microcomputers. It is thus possible to run textual analysis, dictionary, and concordance programs for the Homeric texts on several microcomputers. These programs are explained in Abercrombie's new book, *Computer Programs for Literary Analysis*; for a nominal fee, the publisher will mail a disk containing these programs in Basic.

Those interested in Homeric research can be further served by University MicroComputers (1259 El Camino Real, No. 170, Menlo Park, CA 94025), which produces AcademicFont. This product converts the IBM-PC from a computer displaying one alphabet—English—to one that can display and print both English and Greek. This company also produces a variety of programs for literary research on the computer, specifically for those interested in classical languages and literature.

Critical and Reference Works: Survey Results

To teach the *Iliad* and the *Odyssey* effectively, instructors need to familiarize themselves with available critical, background, and reference works. Asked to name the five to ten most essential works, survey participants listed the following titles most frequently: Albert Lord, *The Singer of Tales*; C. H. Whitman, *Homer and the Heroic Tradition*; M. I. Finley, *The World of Odysseus*; Denys Page, *History of the Homeric* Iliad; Alan Wace and Frank Stubbings, *A Companion to Homer*; G. S. Kirk, *The Songs of Homer*; Milman Parry, *The Making of Homeric Verse*; H. W. Clarke, *The Art of the* Odyssey; James Redfield, *Nature and Culture in the* Iliad; Charles Beye, *The* Iliad, *the* Odyssey, *and the Epic Tradition*; and C. H. Taylor, Jr., *Essays on the* Odyssey: *Selected Modern Criticism*.

Asked to name the scholars with whose works instructors should be most familiar, survey participants noted the following most frequently (the works recommended are in parentheses): Albert Lord (*The Singer of Tales*); Denys Page (*History and the Homeric* Iliad, *The Homeric* Odyssey); C. H. Whitman (*Homer and the Heroic Tradition*); M. I. Finley (*The World of Odysseus*); G. S. Kirk (*The Songs of Homer, Homer and the Oral Tradition, Myth: Its Meanings and Functions in Ancient and Other Cultures, The Nature of Greek Myths*); Alan Wace and Frank Stubbings (*A Companion to Homer*); Milman Parry (*The Making of Homeric Verse*); C. M. Bowra (*Ancient Greek Literature, The Greek Experience, Heroic Poetry, Homer, Oxford Book of Greek Verse, Tradition and Design in the* Iliad); H. W. Clarke (*The Art of the* Odyssey, *Homer's Readers, Twentieth Century Interpretations of* The Odyssey); and James Redfield (*Nature and Culture in the* Iliad).

The Instructor's Library

This section addresses primarily the nonspecialist who teaches Homer in survey and general literature courses. At the same time, however, it provides the classics scholar with at least the most important sources in English for Homeric research. Although much important and ground-breaking work has been done and continues to be done on Homer in languages other than English—especially in German, French, and Greek—only works available in English have been included here. Recommended readings reflect the author's views, based on the number of times works are referred to in Homeric scholarship and on the esteem in which they are held by other Homerists and readers of Homer. The focus is on critically acclaimed Homeric materials available after 1977 since Homeric bibliographies up to 1977 are already available in book form and in journals. This presentation of recent Homeric scholarship should thus not be considered exhaustive but merely an attempt to bring knowledge of Homeric materials up to date. For expediency in reference and utilization, sources have been divided into six categories—bibliographies, translations of Homer into English, guides to the Homeric epics, journals in which Homeric criticism appears, reference works and background studies, and selected critical works in collections of essays, books on Homer, and periodical literature.

Bibliographies

For earlier Homeric materials (1930–70), David W. Packard and Tania Meyers's *Bibliography of Homeric Scholarship* is perhaps the most complete source. The references cited are based on annual citations in *L'Année Philologique* (*APh*), which the authors expanded wherever possible. A planned revision of this bibliography will incorporate material cited in *APh* from 1914 to 1930 and will integrate bibliographies published by Mette, Lesky, and others. A helpful feature of the Packard-Meyer bibliography is its subject index, which divides the sources included into sixteen categories: (1) Language, (2) Meter, (3) Poetics, (4) Composition, (5) Ancient Scholarship, (6) Archaeology and Realien, (7) Art, (8) History, (9) Geography, (10) Homeric Society, (11) Psychology and World-View, (12) Religion, (13) Heroes and Heroines, (14) Individual Episodes, (15) Influence, and (16) Modern Scholarship. For materials since 1970, James P. Holoka's "Homer Studies 1971–1977" strives "to produce an exhaustive chronicle of scholarship in all areas of Homer studies over a limited number of years." Holoka's work is divided into eight major categories with three to seven subtopics each: (1) Preliminary

Declarations, (2) Editions, Commentaries, and Translations, (3) Homer, (4) The *Iliad*, (5) The *Odyssey*, (6) Ancient Scholarship, Scholia, Papyri, and Paleography, (7) History and Archaeology, and (8) Homer and Aftertimes.

A third bibliographical source of interest to students of Homer is *L'Année Philologique* itself, an annual international bibliography of classical and related studies. Fundamental to Homeric research and study, clearly organized, and thoroughly researched, this French publication does not require one to know French in order to use it. Of additional interest are the Homer bibliographies periodically published in the journal *Lustrum* (vols. 1, 1956; 2, 1957; 11, 1966; 15, 1970); E. R. Dodds's "Homer" in *Fifty Years of Classical Scholarship*, edited by Maurice Plantauer; and F. M. Combellack's "Contemporary Homeric Scholarship: Sound or Fury?" For those especially interested in oral literature and its theory, Edward R. Haymes's *Bibliography of Studies Relating to Parry's and Lord's Oral Theory* should be consulted. This work lists some five hundred books, articles, and dissertations that emanated from the work of Milman Parry and Albert B. Lord in the field of oral theory. For the nonspecialist and those teaching in translation, mention should be made of the well-selected and amply annotated bibliography in Kenneth John Atchity's book *Homer's* Iliad. Myrsiades's "Bibliographical Guide to Teaching the Homeric Epics in College Courses" emphasizes translations, background materials, and criticism since 1970 and may be more accessible to the generalist.

Translations

Selection of the appropriate translation of the *Iliad* or *Odyssey* requires that certain issues be raised concerning Homeric verse. A major difficulty in translating from Homeric Greek is the dactylic hexameter line of six feet, in which each foot is made up of three syllables, one long and two short. This line, however, can vary in the final foot by the omission of a syllable or the replacement of a dactyl by a spondee. When in 1911 Cotterill undertook a translation of the *Odyssey* in English hexameter, he discovered that to represent Homer's meter in English he had to invent compound words and to pad his lines with numerous "the"s and "that"s. Other translators (Philip Stanhoe Worsley, William Cowper, William Cullen Bryant, Richmond Lattimore, Robert Fitzgerald) have experimented with meters suited to the English language with equally frustrating results.

A second difficulty lies in the sound and syntax of Homeric Greek, which has its own phonetic intensives, triggering the meaning of a line or verse through its sound before denotative meanings of its formal language can even be considered. The word order of Homeric Greek, its pauses and emphases, presents an equally challenging problem for the English language translator, for the syntax of English does not fairly represent the characteristic fluidity of Greek, a language in which word order can be manipulated in manifold ways. Finally, the morphology of written Greek and its disposition on the page creates an aesthetic meaning tied to the pictograms and ideograms of the ancient Near East, an aesthetic meaning that the Latin alphabet cannot approach in complexity and symbolic beauty.

Thus before selecting a translation for classroom use, the instructor must consider the problems faced by the translator who must create a third artificial language standing between the world of the original and the world of the key languages. The translator is torn between meaning, on the one hand, and the demands of rhythm, sound, and tone, on the other. In verse the dilemma is intensified, for tone is inseparable from meter and one cannot be sacrificed without a concomitant sacrifice in the other. Because tone is the gestural or interpretive aspect of denotative meaning, the translator is placed in an Odyssean bind, between a linguistic Skylla and Charybdis.

There still remains the problem of age. Archaic Greek, charming and strangely familiar from the perspective of modern Greek, is merely unwieldy in translation. To update the language is to assume the equivalency of past and present; to translate into archaic English is to identify two vastly different cultures. What kind of text, then, best serves the modern reader?

At present a number of relatively successful translations (most available in paperback) exist for both the *Iliad* and the *Odyssey*. Before deciding on a particular text, however, one would do well to consult some of the essays on translating Homer. The classic essay on what to expect of a translation of Homer is still Matthew Arnold's *On Translating Homer*, published in London in 1861. Perhaps the most informative essay on translating the *Odyssey* in particular is Howard Clarke's "Translation and Translations," in the appendix to his *Art of the* Odyssey (100–09). Clarke compares Greek with English verse and considers various translations of the *Odyssey*, pointing out the positive and negative points of each. He provides a summary discussion of Homer's meter and suggests the numerous problems the translator must face in rendering his verse into English. Conny Nelson's "Translations of the *Odyssey*," in the now out-of-print *Homer's* Odyssey: *A Critical Handbook* (196–97), supplies an annotated list of twentieth-century translations of the *Odyssey*, comments on the merits of each, and lists important translations of previous times. Robert Fitzgerald's "Postscript to a Translation of the *Odyssey*" (which first appeared in the Anchor edition of his translation only to be omitted in later editions) is a valuable guide to translating the *Odyssey* and to the problems of translation in general. This essay, now available in *The Craft and Context of Translation*, is as much a background on Homer and his work as it is a discussion of translation. Dealing largely with his impressions of the *Odyssey* while translating, Fitzgerald stresses that one's frame of mind in approaching the Homeric world is as important as one's knowledge of Homeric Greek.

Guy Davenport's review of Richmond Lattimore's translation of the *Odyssey*, titled "Another Odyssey," provides illustrations of the great variety of meanings that can be extracted from the same line by different translators. Davenport's essay offers a modest comparison of particular passages and demonstrates several ways in which translators use language to interpret rather than to reveal the original text. Another essay treating the *Odyssey* and its English translators is Robert Fagles's "Homer and Writers." The most recent essay on translating Homer—Walter Shewring's "On Translation" in the epilogue of his prose translation of the *Odyssey* (299–330)— makes a case for translating Homer in prose. His purpose is "to discuss at some length the difficulties of translation in general and of Homeric translation particularly, speaking first of all to the many readers who are well at home with English idiom but have little acquaintance with foreign languages" (299). He succeeds admirably, commenting in the process on several translations of Homer.

Today the Homer instructor can select from a variety of contemporary translations, most of which are available in paperback editions. The verse version of the *Odyssey* considered closest to Homer's original line is Richmond Lattimore's, although critics prefer his *Iliad* to his *Odyssey*. Robert Fitzgerald's version, by contrast, seems to lose in accuracy what it gains in freeness and raciness. Another attempt to turn this epic into English verse and yet remain literal is Albert Cook's version, published by Norton in two different editions—by itself and in the Norton Critical Edition, which includes background materials and criticism as well as the translation. Cook's translation is more likely to find favor among those who find Lattimore's too scholarly and stiff and Fitzgerald's too loose and free. Cedric H. Whitman feels Fitzgerald's translation to be more beautiful but says that "Cook's may prove to be easier to teach from in Humanities courses and his verses are regularly clean and readable."

Two more verse translations deserve mention, the first available in paperback and the second a hardback. Ennis Rees's version attempts to recreate the original, a goal he shares with translators like Chapman and Pope but which he believes has been neglected since the eighteenth century both in theory and in practice. Rees claims to be faithful to the sentiments, ideas, and images of the original in attempting a readable English poem. Moreover, he says in his introduction:

> In diction I have aimed at effective expression in the large area between
> the stilted and the vulgar and always with regard to dramatic context.
> In meter the line I have found best suited for rendering the original

dactylic hexameters is a loose measure of five major stresses plus a varying number of relatively unaccented syllables.   (xv)

Denison Bingham Hull tries in his version to accomplish Matthew Arnold's objectives by composing his translation "in the English spoken by educated people. It is simple and direct, tends to be paratactic rather than syntactic, just as Homer does, and is made up of plain and simple words" (Homer's *Odyssey* xii–xiii). Those interested in studying the Greek epic tradition might find an advantage in using Hull's translation, for he has also translated the *Iliad* and the Byzantine epic *Digenis Akritas*.

Homer's epics have been translated into prose as frequently as into verse. The most recent and the most successfully rendered prose version is Walter Shewring's *Odyssey*. The best-selling prose translation, however, is still E. V. Rieu's with its urbane and lucid language. T. E. Shaw's prose version uses language that is less Homer than Shaw. W. H. D. Rouse, who translated the *Odyssey* as a novel, creates an impression of the twentieth-century Anglo-Saxon world rather than the Greek one of three thousand years ago. Older editions still available in paperback include the translations of George Herbert Palmer, Samuel Butler, and S. H. Butcher and A. Lang.

As for the *Iliad*, the best-known and most admired verse translation is Richmond Lattimore's, generally accepted as the best in English. Robert Fitzgerald's verse version, published in 1974, follows the same tradition as that exemplified in his *Odyssey*, although most critics would agree that as an English poem his *Odyssey* is more successful than his *Iliad*. Ennis Rees's version of the *Iliad*, like his *Odyssey*, attempts to recreate the original. A recent verse translation not yet available in paperback is Denison B. Hull's *Iliad*.

The most successfully rendered prose translations of the *Iliad* are those of E. V. Rieu, in the same clear prose as his *Odyssey*, and W. H. D. Rouse, the colloquial prose of which is intended to be appropriate to "the world's greatest war novel," as the Mentor Classic paperback edition unabashedly claims. The version by Alston Hurd Chase and William G. Perry, Jr., attempts, according to their preface, to correct previous abuses with a translation that "shall neither lose Homeric rapidity through archaism nor sacrifice Homeric dignity to a slick colloquialism." This straightforward translation does indeed avoid archaisms and colloquialisms, but at the same time it lacks color.

Guides

Line-by-line guides keyed to English translations exist only for the *Iliad*. Three such works are available at present, all in paperback editions. Malcolm M. Willcock's *A Companion to the* Iliad, based on Richmond Latti-more's translation, is intended for the general reader who has little familiarity with the historic details, mythological allusions, and Homeric conventions encountered on first reading the epic. In a companion volume by Willcock, *A Commentary on Homer's* Iliad, *Books I–VI*, the greater attention paid to the original Greek makes this supplementary text a useful aid to those reading the *Iliad* in the original. A third guide, James C. Hogan's *A Guide to the* Iliad, is keyed to the Fitzgerald translation. Hogan provides an excellent introduction to the cultural setting, style, and poetry of the *Iliad*, followed by a short summary and a line-by-line commentary on each book. A more recent commentary on the *Iliad*, available for the first four books and only in a hardback edition, is volume 1 of G. S. Kirk's *The* Iliad: *A Commentary*.

One of the most complete commentaries on the *Iliad*, E. T. Owen's *The Story of the* Iliad is an older guide, commenting book by book. Its lively and intelligent commentary treats narrative technique, imagery, and characterization for each of the twenty-four books. Mention should also be made of C. W. Macleod's *Homer*: Iliad, *Book XXIV*, which contains an excellent introduction to Homer's poem—in particular to his language, style, meter, and prosody—followed by the Greek text of book 24 and copious line-by-line commentary on this central book of the *Iliad*.

Guides to the *Odyssey* for the general reader are not available. However, W. B. Stanford's two-volume edition of the epic has an excellent introduction to the story and characters of the epic, the nature and style of Homer's poetry, the Homeric problem, Homeric geography, the Homeric house, the Homeric ship, the people of the Homeric age, and Mykenaian Greek. The greater part of each volume is devoted to line-by-line commentary on Homer's language as well as on explication of Homer's text. Howard W. Clarke's *The Art of the* Odyssey is regarded by its author as "an essay in literary explication" and can be used as a guide for the general reader. The book is divided into five chapters covering book 1, the Telemachy, Odysseus's adventures, Odysseus's return, and a comparison of the *Iliad* and the *Odyssey*. Included are three excellent appendixes on chronology, translations of the *Odyssey*, and further readings.

In addition to these two texts, a number of works contain short, concise essays on specific passages in the *Odyssey*. The first of these, and the only one available in paperback, is D. M. Gaunt's *Surge and Thunder: Critical Readings in Homer's* Odyssey. It presents twenty passages in the author's prose translation followed by "Appreciation" sections, which express the sensations the author experienced in reading the original. Although dated, W. J. Woodhouse's *Composition of Homer's* Odyssey provides interesting discussions in a light and amusing style on virtually all the episodes of the *Odyssey*. Denys Page in his *Folktales in Homer's* Odyssey devotes his entire work to a discussion of the tales that occupy books 9–12, stressing Homer's ability to infuse existing folktales with life and realism and to make them his own; he finds Homer comparable to Shakespeare in his personalization of borrowed materials. In the same vein, Agathe Thornton's *People and Themes in Homer's Odyssey* provides an informative, educative treatment of the Telemachy, which she views as the preparation of Telemachos to perform as his father's son. Her study is interesting as well for her comments on books 5–6. Here she notes that the Kalypso and the Phaiakian adventures are the only ones described by Homer himself rather than by Odysseus in flashback; her objective is to demonstrate they are the only original myths in the *Odyssey*.

Journals

Much of what is new in Homeric studies can be found in a large number of journals whose articles range from archaeological, linguistic, and comparative studies to interpretative essays on the epics. It is not the purpose of this essay to update earlier Homeric bibliographies. Its intention, rather, is to provide a selective guide to post-1978 materials, a period for which a Homeric bibliography does not yet exist. What follows is a list of the ten journals that since 1978 have published a number of interpretative or explicative essays on each of the two epics or on specific books of each epic—articles that, in the author's opinion, instructors of the *Iliad* and the *Odyssey* would find useful. The number following each journal title indicates the percentage of the total number of articles on Homer published in these periodicals since 1978.

   American Journal of Philology (21%), *Transactions of the American Philological Association* (13%), *Classical Bulletin* (10%), *Classical Quarterly* (10%), *Greece and Rome* (10%), *Classical Philology* (9%), *Journal of Hellenic Studies* (9%), *Hermes* (6%), *Mnemosyne* (6%), and *Ramus* (6%).

Reference Works and Background Studies

Although there are numerous sources for background information, only a few have exercised wide influence. One of the most reliable and useful of these, *A Companion to Homer*, edited by Alan J. B. Wace and Frank H. Stubbings, represents a teacher's most important single source for background material on Homer and his epics. It treats all aspects of Homeric scholarship, although its discussions tend to be dry and sometimes overly erudite. Part 1, "The Homeric Poems and Their Authorship," contains essays on the poems (meter, style, composition, language of Homer, and Homer and other epic poetry) and on Homeric criticism (transmission of the text and the Homeric question). Part 2, "The Picture and the Record," includes sections on the setting (the physical geography of Greece and the Aegean, lands and people in Homer, and Aegean languages of the heroic age), on the rediscovery of the heroic world (the history of Homeric archaeology, the early age of Greece, and the principal Homeric sites), on social culture (polity and society, religion, and burial customs), and on material culture (houses and palaces, dress, arms and armour, food and agriculture, crafts and industries, communications and trade, and writing). Another influential work is M. I. Finley's *The World of Odysseus*, a background study of early Greek society that examines such topics as the class structure of Homer's world; the sources of its wealth, morals, and values; and the relation of household to community. Whereas Finley's work lays the groundwork for understanding Homer's physical universe, yet another excellent work, George Thomson's *Studies in Ancient Greek Society*, interprets that universe from the Marxist point of view, concluding in part 5 that Homer's epics emerged spontaneously from the daily lives, chants, and songs of the laboring class. Two other works on history and religion deserve mention. Denys Page's *History and the Homeric Iliad* discusses the Greeks and their culture in the thirteenth century BC, while Martin P. Nilsson's *Homer and Mycenae* traces the relation between Homer and Mykenaian civilization. Somewhat outdated, both of these works are now classics in their areas.

Greek thought and its evolution are explored from the vantage point of the Homeric epics in John H. Finley's *Four Stages of Greek Thought*. Bruno Snell's classic *The Discovery of the Mind: The Greek Origins of European Thought* probes Homer's view of humanity and nature and argues for the poem's composition before the invention of a written language. The way in which ideas are treated in Homer is discussed in a number of works that, although not exclusively on Homer, have had a great influence on Homeric studies. E. R. Dodds's *The Greeks and the Irrational* brings together evidence on an important and relatively unfamiliar aspect of the mental world of ancient Greece, the role of primitive and irrational forces in Greek society. Eric A. Havelock in *Preface to Plato* demonstrates the growth of early Greek thought, while Hugh Lloyd-Jones in *The Justice of Zeus* sketches the nature of *Dike* from the Homeric epics to the end of the fifth century BC. Victorino Tejera in *Modes of Greek Thought* expounds on the thesis that the intelligibility, naturalness, and monumentality of Homer and other Greek authors make them enduring and great.

Together with works on the physical world and early thought that define the scholarly context of the Homeric epics, several works on the oral tradition have exerted an inordinate influence on Homeric criticism. Among them, one would have to select Milman Parry's essays on Homeric meter and the nature of oral composition, collected in *The Making of Homeric Verse: The Collected Papers of Milman Parry*; Albert B. Lord's *The Singer of Tales*; G. S. Kirk's *Homer and the Epic*, the shortened version of Kirk's *The Songs of Homer*; and Rhys Carpenter's *Folk Tale, Fiction, and Saga in the Homeric Epics*. Milman Parry's essays have had the greatest influence in defining the nature of Homer's art and are thus of great historical significance. The bulk of the material in Lord's work deals with Homer's oral formulas, which Lord compares to modern Yugoslavian oral epics to establish a related oral tradition. The work is most helpful as a guide to understanding oral style and language and their importance to the *Iliad* and the *Odyssey*. Kirk's work provides background material on the oral epic, examines Homer's language and epic formulas, and contains a sizable essay on each epic. Carpenter's work includes a chapter of particular interest in which the author argues that both the *Odyssey* and the old English epic *Beowulf* are based in part on the folktale of the bear's son. A more approachable study to Homer's oral poetry and epic technique, with long chapters explicating the two epics, is Charles Rowan Beye's *The* Iliad, *the* Odyssey, *and the Epic Tradition*; published in 1966, it incorporates in its reading of Homer the then most recent archaeological, linguistic, and literary research. More recent studies of Homer's oral art that correct many of the erroneous assumptions held in earlier books are Michael Nagler's *Spontaneity and Tradition: A Study in the Oral Art of Homer* and Minna Skafte Jensen's *Homeric Question and the Oral-Formulaic Theory*.

One classic work worthy of mention for its background material as well as for its textual criticism is *Homer Revisited* by the Greek Homerist Johannes Kakridis. This collection of ten studies written over a twenty-year period reflects Kakridis's views on both the *Iliad* and the *Odyssey* as they affect a variety of topics: problems of the Homeric Helen, the role of women in the *Iliad*, Homer's philhellenism, double repetitions in Homer, the motif of the god-sent mist in the *Iliad*, imagined ecphrases, the first scene with Chryses in the *Iliad*, the simile in *Iliad* 2.259–67, Nausikaa, and the recognition of Odysseus. Another classic work of interest is Arthur W. H. Adkins's *Merit and Responsibility: A Study in Greek Values*, which brings together the research of the author's doctoral thesis submitted in the spring of 1957. Using a limited range of Greek words, Adkins demonstrates certain relationships between Greek values and Greek society. J. T. Sheppard's *The Pattern of the* Iliad is also regarded as a classic work on Homer, largely for its approach to reading the poetry of the *Iliad* without questioning the epic's origins and background.

For those seeking a concise account of Homeric scholarship covering all aspects of the Homeric poems, the third chapter of the classical historian Albin Lesky's *A History of Greek Literature* is an excellent beginning, although somewhat outdated. In addition, Hermann Ferdinand Frankel's *Early Greek Poetry and Philosophy* covers the oral singer, language, verse, style, epic material, the gods, Homeric man, and a discussion of the *Odyssey* as an end product of the oral tradition. C. A. Trypanis's *The Homeric Epics* is a more recent introduction summarizing previous Homeric scholarship. Trypanis, the Bywater and Sotheby Professor of Byzantine and Modern Greek Languages and Literature at Oxford, professor of classics at Chicago University, and currently minister of culture and science in the Greek government, wrote this 108-page introduction to the Homeric poems to help Greek schoolmasters acquaint themselves with the epics. It is intended to summarize the vast material available on Homer for those without access to library resources or incapable of reading the languages in which much Homeric commentary is written. Another short introduction to Homer (108 pages) that tries to summarize much of modern scholarship on the epics is W. A. Camps's *An Introduction to Homer*. Its primary purpose, however, is the effectiveness of the epics' poetic art and the enjoyment derived from reading these works in translation. Jasper Griffin in his *Homer* has produced a 78-page essay on those ideas of the two epics that have had a profound influence on the thought and literature of the West. Howard Clarke's *Homer's Readers* is another recent nontechnical introduction to Homer's poems for those who know these epics primarily in English translation and want to know more about them as historical documents and literary monuments. This introduction offers the reader a historical survey of the fashions of Homeric criticism from medieval times to the present. Another introduction deserves mention as the last book written by the great classicist Maurice Bowra before his death in 1971. Nine chapters of *Homer* were posthumously discovered among his papers, five of which were considered ready for the printer while four still needed minor revisions. Hugh Lloyd-Jones undertook the task of putting the chapters on oral composition, the Greek heroic age, epic formulas, similes, and the Homeric question in a publishable form. Of all the concise accounts, only Bowra and Clarke are unavailable in paperback.

Two works serve the double function of providing background material and literary criticism on the Homeric epics; they are Cedric H. Whitman's *Homer and the Heroic Tradition* and T. B. L. Webster's *From Mycenae to Homer*. Whitman's book attempts to integrate archaeology, linguistics, history, anthropology, oral literature, and literary criticism as they relate to Homer, and it offers an analysis of the *Iliad* based on the epic's imagery. The most important aspect of this work, however, remains its thought-provoking chapters on geometric art and the application of that art to the epics. Webster's book uses our new knowledge of Michael Ventris's decipherment of Linear B in 1952 to describe Greek art and poetry in the periods preceding and including that of Homer (see Chadwick, *Decipherment of Linear B*).

Those instructors of Homer interested in updating their audiovisual materials for the epics should consult the two articles by Elizabeth E. Seittelman that recently appeared in *Classical World*.

Critical Studies

Collections of Essays

The most readily available collection of essays dealing with both epics is still *Homer: A Collection of Critical Essays*, edited by George Steiner and Robert Fagles. Unfortunately, many of the selections in this collection are no more than notes or poems on Homeric characters and themes, included because they represent the work of well-known scholars or famous poets. As a scholarly effort, the book is worthwhile for its inclusion of essays by W. B. Stanford, G. E. Dimock, Jr., and Eric Auerbach on the *Odyssey*; and by Cedric Whitman, Albert Lord, and Rachel Bespaloff on the *Iliad*. The introduction by George Steiner, "Homer and the Scholars," gives a succinct summary of the main preoccupations of twentieth-century scholars concerning the Homeric epics; Robert Fagles in the epilogue, "Homer and the Writers," discusses the *Odyssey* and its English translators. *Approaches to Homer*, edited by Carl A. Rubino and Cynthia W. Shelmerdine, is a more recent collection that emphasizes the variety of approaches distinguishing Homeric scholarship today. This collection of nine essays by well-known classicists approaches the epics from the perspectives of archaeology, economic history, philosophy, literary criticism, linguistics, and Byzantine history. In his *Homer: Tradition and Invention*, Bernard C. Fenik has edited a collection of essays outlining the state of Homeric studies and recent trends in Homeric scholarship. Consisting of five lectures delivered at a University of Cincinnati classics symposium held in March 1976, the text includes Alfred Heubeck's "Homeric Studies Today: Results and Prospects"; G. S. Kirk's "The Formula Duels in Books 3 and 7 of the *Iliad*"; J. B. Hainsworth's "Good and Bad Formulae"; Uvo Hoelscher's "The Transformation from Folk-tale to Epic"; and Bernard Fenik's "Stylization and Variety: Four Monologues in the *Iliad*." Several interesting essays on Homer by Cedric H. Whitman are also to be found in a recent collection on Greek literature edited by Charles Segal, *The Heroic Paradox: Essays on Homer, Sophocles, and Aristophanes*.

Eight contemporary essays devoted entirely to the *Iliad* are collected in *Essays on the* Iliad: *Selected Modern Criticism*, edited by John Wright. This edition, available in paperback, includes studies by Adam Parry, J. B. Hainsworth, Joseph Russo and Bennett Simon, M. M. Willock, Norman Austin, James M. Redfield, E. T. Owen, and Martin Mueller. The essays embrace the whole range of issues raised by critics in this century, moving from the basic question of textual authenticity to problems of Homeric narrative and close textual analysis of selected scenes. Rachel Bespaloff's *On the* Iliad contains seven essays translated from the French by Mary McCarthy. Bespaloff links the Homeric epics with biblical prophecy, a task that adds a significantly Kierkegaardian tone to her commentary and provides a number of unique, although somewhat dated (1947), insights. Mention should also be made of two well-known and influential essays on the *Iliad*. The first, a much-anthologized essay, is Simone Weil's *The* Iliad: *Or, The Poem of Force*. Weil sees the *Iliad* as a tale of power and hate in which overwhelming pessimism is resisted by men and women who can still feel normal human impulses. The second is Richmond Lattimore's introduction to his translation of the *Iliad*. In this forty-five-page essay, Lattimore provides a concise summary that includes background material on Homer's age, his style, the epic cycle, the legend of Troy, and character studies of Hektor, Achilleus, Agamemnon, and Aias.

The most recent collection of critical essays on the *Odyssey* is *Twentieth Century Interpretations of* The Odyssey, edited by Howard W. Clarke. It includes Richmond Lattimore's introduction to his translation of the *Odyssey* in addition to a number of other insightful essays, including Charles W. Eckert's on Telemachos, W. B. Stanford's on Odysseus's heroism (excerpted from *The Ulysses Theme*), Cedric H. Whitman's on changes in the *Odyssey*, Jasper Griffin's on Homeric characterization, Frederick M. Combellack's on the bow contest, and Dorothea Wender's on the epic's controversial ending. The Norton Critical Edition of the *Odyssey* contains not only a verse translation of the epic by Albert Cook but a section entitled "Backgrounds and Sources" that provides information on language, history, culture, poetic conventions, and composition of the poem. A second section, "The *Odyssey* in Antiquity," offers critical commentaries on the poem from ancient and medieval times. The last section, "Criticism," includes pieces by Racine, Goethe, Ezra Pound, G. E. Dimock, Jr., Gabriel Germain, T. W. Adorno, Cedric H. Whitman, Anne Amory, Albert Cook, John H. Finley, Jr., Charles Segal, Paolo Vivante, Edwin Dolin, Charles Doria, and Clement Goodson.

Another representative collection is *Essays on the* Odyssey: *Selected Modern Criticism*, edited by Charles H. Taylor, Jr. Each of the volume's seven essays, according to the editor's introduction, "suggests in its own terms some of the reasons for the *Odyssey*'s extraordinarily durable appeal. Together, they should send the reader back to the poem with a heightened awareness of its significance." The first essay, by W. K. C. Guthrie, treats the Homeric gods; W. B. Stanford discourses on the figures confronted by Odysseus on his travels; George de F. Lord argues for Odysseus as a hero in need of rehabilitation before his return to Ithaka; George E. Dimock, Jr., deals with the meanings of Odysseus's name; William S. Anderson compares the worlds of Elysium and Ogygia; Charles H. Taylor, Jr., treats the diversity of Odysseus's adventures; and Anne Amory deals with Penelope's recognition of her husband before he is fully acknowledged.

No longer in print, *Homer's* Odyssey: *A Critical Handbook*, edited by Conny Nelson, covers a wide spectrum of opinions and contains some of the most perceptive essays written on the *Odyssey*. The editor divides the work into five sections: "Homer's Characters" (essays by W. B. Stanford, Charles H. Taylor, Jr., Howard W. Clarke, and J. W. Mackail); "Homer's Universe" (M. I. Finley and G. M. A. Grube); "The *Odyssey*: Epic Style and Epic Form" (Erich Auerbach and Denys Page); "The *Odyssey*: Themes and Structures" (Frank W. Jones, Edward F. D'Arms, Karl K. Hulley, and Walter Morris Hart); and "The *Odyssey*: Three Contemporary Interpretations" (L. A. Post, George E. Dimock, Jr., and George de F. Lord). The editor includes lists of further readings, translations, and a pronunciation guide.

Book-Length Studies

In the past decade a number of books on Homer's epics have been published by a new generation of classical scholars who have both questioned the work of their predecessors and added to it. These books are especially valuable to the nonspecialist looking for good literary criticism on the epics that takes into consideration the most recent developments and directions of Homeric scholarship. The earliest of these books is James M. Redfield's *Nature and Culture in the* Iliad: *The Tragedy of Hector*, which, as its title indicates, examines this epic by focusing on Hektor. Largely unitarian in approach, Redfield develops his work in two directions: the *Iliad* as a unified work of art and Homeric society as a functioning cultural system. A second work, Norman Austin's *Archery at the Dark of the Moon: Poetic Problems in Homer's* Odyssey, treats Homer as a mature poet rather than a stylistic primitive. Through an analysis of Homeric formulas and Homeric concepts, Austin highlights the maturity and intelligence of Homer's carefully posted signs that guide us through the epic and argues against those who would see these signs as mechanical instruments for transmitting oral tales. Gregory Nagy in *The Best of the Achaeans: Concepts of the Hero in Archaic Greek Poetry* deals with the problem of heroes in cults and heroes in the epic. This work on the *Iliad* serves as a primer on the concept of the hero in classical Greek civilization and on the poetic forms that are used to define that hero. W. Thomas MacCary in *Childlike Achilles: Ontogeny and Phylogeny in the* Iliad interprets the *Iliad* from a somewhat different critical perspective, a psychoanalytic viewpoint. As MacCary states in his preface:

> I have determined to situate the relevant precepts of Freudian and post-Freudian psychology (basically the theory of narcissism and "mir-

roring") within the Western philosophical tradition, with its attempts to describe the process through which the individual locates himself in his time and culture.

A recent work on the *Odyssey*, Jenny Strauss Clay's *The Wrath of Athena: Gods and Men in the* Odyssey, takes as its guiding principal the fact that Homer can only be interpreted through Homer. Clay's volume begins with an examination of the proem and proceeds to the relation between the divine and the human in the *Odyssey*. The remaining chapters deal with these relations from various perspectives. Two recent works on the *Iliad* address themselves more directly to the nonspecialist reader who studies or teaches this epic in translation. The first, Seth L. Schein's literary study *The Mortal Hero*, is grounded in technical scholarship and intends "to interpret the poem as much as possible on its own mythological, religious, ethical, and artistic terms." The work contains a chapter on the poetic tradition that gave rise to the *Iliad* and provides criticism on the gods, war, death, heroism, Achilleus, and Hektor. The second work, Martin Mueller's *The* Iliad, was written for the Unwin Critical Library, whose aim is to devote volumes to single major texts in order "to provide a scholarly introduction and a stimulus to critical thought and discussion." Mueller's work includes commentary on the *Iliad*'s plot, particularly its battles, and has sections on the simile, the gods, the Homeric question, and the *Iliad*'s influence on later ages. Another useful introduction to the *Iliad* for both the specialist and nonspecialist is Kenneth John Atchity's *Homer's* Iliad: *The Shield of Memory*. Atchity, laying the Homeric question aside, is more concerned with treating the *Iliad* as a literary masterpiece by focusing on its beauty and profundity through a close analysis of the poem, its themes, and its images. As he states in the introduction, his book is

> a reexamination of the *Iliad*, focusing on images of artifacts, such as the great shield, which serve as signposts in the vast but coherent landscape that shapes character, action, and symbolism into a clear expression of Homer's instructive theme. That theme is the relationship between order and disorder, on all levels, from the most personal to the most widely social, from the human to the divine.

Like Atchity's work, Jasper Griffin's *Homer on Life and Death* tries to avoid discussing the Homeric question and the formulaic theory of the poems— issues that have dominated analyses of these epics in the past forty years— and instead focuses on the literary merits of Homer's works. Although Griffin explores the literary uniqueness of both epics as the embodiment of "a clear and unique vision of the world, of heroism, and of life and death," he nevertheless operates from the assumption that such a vision can only belong to a single mind.

Three books published in the past decade by Homerists of an earlier generation also deserve mention. The first, *Homer's* Odyssey by John H. Finley, Jr., offers insights on this epic by a well-known teacher of the classics. In this important but difficult book, Finley explores the unity of design in the *Odyssey* to show the connection between the actions of three principal characters—Penelope, Telemachos, and Odysseus. The second, Paolo Vivante's *The Epithets in Homer: A Study in Poetic Values*, argues that Homeric epithets occur based on reasons intrinsic to the value of the expressions made rather than on any external frame of reference. The third, *Homer*, also by Vivante, is a general study that concentrates on Homer's poetic treatment of story, characters, and nature rather than on the place of the epics in the oral tradition, a more common approach.

A series of critical studies, Mnemosyne Bibliotheca Classica Batava, published by E. J. Brill in the Netherlands, is worthy of mention because it has been regularly issuing volumes on Homer since the early seventies. These books, written by both English-speaking and foreign scholars, are presented in English and deal with a variety of rather specific and somewhat esoteric topics, ranging from the theme of the mutilation of the corpse in the *Iliad*, the arms of Achilleus, and the last scenes of the *Odyssey* to a study of Homeric epithets, the oral nature of the Homeric simile, and manners in the Homeric epic (see Mnemosyne).

Homeric scholarship in the twentieth century has been divided between two camps: the unitarians, who believe that the Homeric epics were written by one person, or at least that each as a complete whole was written by a single author; and the analysts, who view the Homeric epics as mere compilations of preexisting stories, or at best as works of a single mind coordinating the contributions of other minds before the works were set down in the form in which they now exist. This scholarship has been unduly preoccupied with the question of authorship, what has been referred to as the Homeric question. That the Homeric question is significant is undeniable. It raises the issues of inconsistencies in language, equipment, religious practices, and social customs between the two epics; the possibility that these epics were based on preexistent tales, songs, or lays, even, perhaps, on older epics; the diverse dating of materials from different periods that the interjoining of the layers of the epics betrays; and the problem of whether the Homeric epics were completed as written or as oral compositions.

Nevertheless, both poems are in the same meter (dactylic hexameter); both are characteristically oral poetry transmitted by recitation (whether they were set down in some symbolic form or not); both were composed at the dawn of Western civilization when abstract thought was barely beginning; and both relied for their preservation on the unlettered, materially preoccupied inhabitants of the Homeric age, a reliance that made necessary a technique (the Homeric simile) and a philosophical system (myth) that concretized the amorphous and made literal the abstract. These elements are more important to the Homer instructor than the disparities within and between the Homeric epics.

The problems the reader of the Homeric epics faces are not, at any rate, unique to either epic. In both epics it is a question of accepting the works as complete in themselves, accepting them either as compilations of diverse materials or as a unique whole, according to one's school of thought. The less seasoned reader is bound to be put off by an archaic language more stilted than our own, by the repetitive requirements of oral poetry, by the characteristics of an age thousands of years removed, by books that seem unrelated to the main themes being developed in the work as a whole, by the interference of meddling gods, and by heroes whose standards of conduct are so different from our own. Readers would do well to put their reservations behind them and plunge headlong into the world of either epic without discrimination.

Part Two

APPROACHES

INTRODUCTION

The seventeen essays collected in this part are written by scholars and teachers representing a cross section of colleges and universities that offer Homer in translation in a variety of departments (English, comparative literature, classics, and history) and in courses ranging from freshman composition to specialized seminars. Included among the essayists are English teachers offering survey and composition courses, classicists offering Homer in introductory courses on the classics, Homerists and classics scholars teaching seminars on the epics, and historians using Homer in introductory history courses.

The essays are divided into two categories. The first, "Teaching Homer and the Homeric Epics," consists of nine contributions that deal with such general topics as backgrounds, influences, and themes common to both epics. Providing a framework for the whole collection, W. McLeod's "The *Iliad* and the *Odyssey* as Great Literature" explores the fundamental question What is great literature? Acknowledging there are no infallible rules for greatness, McLeod nevertheless suggests that an appropriate guideline to greatness is the ability of a work to move the reader. Homer's familiarity with human nature, his universality, and his realism are qualities that stir our emotions and inspire points of contact between the ancient poet and his modern reader. By contrast, Robert Zaslavsky claims that the epics cannot succeed unless, approached on their own terms, they are allowed to speak for and about themselves. Zaslavsky argues that we should preserve the exoticism of Homer's epics rather than seek familiarity, for in that exoticism lies Homer's appeal. J. Frank Papovich, like Zaslavsky, highlights the poet's unfamiliarity, asserting that we are lulled into false confidence once we confuse modern and ancient perspectives and traditions. Rather, it is the original intention of the text that must be preserved. Examining the text through key terms, an approach suggested by A. W. H. Adkins, Papovich leads students to view both descriptive and evaluative usages in transliteration, rather than translation, as a means of experiencing significant but often neglected aspects of the epics.

In "Homeric Epic and the Social Order," Michael N. Nagler argues that the *Odyssey* exists at three levels of semantic organization, each equally valid: stratum, substratum, and universal signification. The first treats identity (for the whole epic can be seen as a recognition scene); the second, experience (the ways in which a human being develops through experience and learns from it); and the third, community (a balance of reciprocal order and disorder).

The roles of the gods and heroes are addressed in two essays: "Homeric

Icons" by Norman Austin and "The Concept of the Hero" by John E. Rexine. Focusing on the Homeric gods, Austin views the forces that motivate human action as critically central to understanding Homer. Indeed, he asks, why read Homer at all if we dismiss these agents of destiny? In his examination of correspondences between human and divine motivation, Austin explores both the contributions of Plato and the relationship of Freud's concept of the ego and superego to Homer's gods and heroes. By contrast, Rexine views the epics through their heroes. Conscious of their humanity and its limitations, Homer's heroes serve as a model for human action and character. They appeal to us, Rexine concludes, because we recognize in them the fullest possibilities of our own humanity.

In "Homer in Art," Howard Clarke surveys pictorial representations of Homeric themes to heighten our reading of the epics through analogous presentational experiences. Toward this end, he discusses a range of artistic reinterpretations of Homer's diverse scenes that bridge, as he says, "with color and line, that mysterious space between the poems and their audience."

The final pair of essays in this section examine approaches to teaching Homer in composition and history classes. George D. Economou, experimenting with the Homeric epic in a freshman honors composition course, assigns daily journal entries of 250 words and a series of formal papers. Using personal experiences, historical issues, comparative study, and textural analysis, Economou demonstrates that both composition and the epics profit from this innovative technique. Ronald P. Legon has committed himself to finding in Homer "all the books you need." He has adopted the world of Homer as the integrating theme in an alternative survey history course. Used as primary source material, the epics become the basis for term papers that evaluate both classical historiography and modern historical approaches to using classical sources.

The second group of essays, "Teaching Specific Epics," focuses on contributions dealing with one epic or a particular aspect of an epic. Two approaches to teaching the *Iliad* open part 2. In the first, Mitzi M. Brunsdale trains future teachers in a world literature survey course for sophomore English majors. Observing that she approaches the *Iliad* "with a sense of inadequacy," Brunsdale explains how she uses a series of critical essays linked to each other thematically, compares various translations of the texts, and draws on period historical sources, following Gilbert Highet's suggested teaching sequence for the *Iliad* in *The Art of Teaching*. In the second essay, Sally MacEwen uses the *Iliad* both to introduce literary history and to explore the meaning of writing and literature. Attaching the ideas of creating and writing first to a real setting, students are then allowed to pursue theoretical issues in terms of three questions: the historical phenomenon of writing, the significance of style, and the power of writing itself.

The next three essays introduce various additional teaching techniques. George E. Dimock follows the practice of *explication de texte*, encouraging his students to read the *Iliad* line by line to expose what he regards as literature's essential function— "to convey what a given human experience might be like." The poet-and-muse agency is most fully understood and experienced, Dimock asserts, by making these feelings accessible to students. Similarly, Barbara Apstein argues that examining a fundamentally alien culture brings students to new realizations about their own customs and habits of mind. The use of the *Odyssey* as a springboard for investigating students' lives not only increases the relevance of the literature course but enhances its function as a significant life experience. Elizabeth A. Fisher presents study questions to elucidate Homer's epic material for classics students. Three prepared sets of questions cover the *Odyssey* by focusing attention on significant issues. Assigned to accompany the readings, the study questions reduce uncertainty about how to approach the text and increase a student's ability to achieve course objectives.

The final three essays present techniques for studying the *Odyssey*. Robert L. Tener addresses student views of the *Odyssey* as a "museum piece" by raising the question What does the *Odyssey* offer a modern reader? Avoiding special lectures on ancient religion and society, Tener keeps the focus on Homer's universal themes, looking for parallels in modern times. He views Homer's hero as an archetypal figure who sets direction by a compass human beings still travel by today. In his essay William C. Scott suggests that instructors should consider teaching the epics by "building down," that is, by beginning with an overall statement on the meaning of the epic and then moving to individual scenes. If an adequate general statement is made initially, all the books of the epic will share in it, and the impressionism that sometimes dominates discussion of the epic can be avoided. In "The Aristotelian Unity of Odysseus's Wanderings," Rick M. Newton makes the point that Homer's poetic treatment of quasi-historical subject matter has a reality that truly imitates life even as the poet's arrangement of Odysseus's adventures follows a philosophical plan.

TEACHING HOMER AND THE HOMERIC EPICS

The *Iliad* and the *Odyssey* as Great Literature

W. McLeod

For the ancient Greeks he was *The* Poet, without qualification and without ambiguity. Later ages provide glowing testimonials: "nothing inappropriate" (Horace), "none better" (the elder Pliny), "Prince of Poets" (Chapman), "loftiness of thought" (Dryden), "all the books you need" (Buckingham), "who most excelled" (Pope), "pure serene" (Keats), "likest a god" (Sainte-Beuve), "strong-wing'd music" (Tennyson), "the greatest poet in the world" (John Cowper Powys). "Securus judicat orbis terrarum," said Augustine, in another context; "If everyone agrees, it must be so." By this axiom alone, Homer ranks as "great literature."

Despite such good notices, today's students see cause to approach Homer with misgivings. After all, he is old, he is long, he is poetry. He does, however, have compensating virtues, which will win over most of those who persevere to read him. To begin with, his lucidity is irresistible ("plain in his words and style, . . . simple in his ideas" [Arnold, *On Translating* 92, 1905 ed.]). It follows that in the classroom exegesis is hardly required. Even so, as teachers we can still find much to say. We can discuss the evidence for his time and place, slight though it be. We can speculate about his audience. We can worry about how his text reached us—Homeridai, Pisistratus, eccentric papyri, and the rest. We can argue that certain books and lines are spurious, if that game appeals to us. We can study the archaeological background and learn to visualize the boar's-tusk helmet. We can pretend he is a historian and use him as a sourcebook for the Late Bronze Age. We can talk about his gods, who at first glance appear omnipotent, or about Fate, which seems to bind even the gods. We can examine Homeric society, as if the poems were social documents. We can ponder the implications of Homer as a traditional poet; this undertaking is a bit more fruitful, for, even apart from uncovering other, more dubious insights, it helps to explain certain textual oddities that in any other author would be emended.

These are all splendid topics, well calculated to take up many hours of classroom time, and some of them are respectable academically. The problem is that they have nothing to do with Homer's greatness.

We can then look at Homer's narrative technique, which at least has the virtue of being intrinsic to his epic. A traditional poet will, of course, restate themes, but this one uses parallels for his own purposes. Homer regularly says one thing while another is on his mind. He contrives parallels by inventing mythological stories, such as the revolt against Zeus in *Iliad* 1 (Willcock, "Mythological" 141). Again, Meleagros is uncannily similar to Achilleus, even to the extent of making Kleo-patra correspond to Patro-klos (Rosner 314). Certain scenes that seem pointless or unnoticed when they first occur gain significance when they recur in a memorable context; they may be called "anticipatory doublets" (Fenik, *Typical* 214). Thus, for no apparent reason Athene kindles a flame from the head of Diomedes (*Il.* 5.4); later she repeats the favor for Achilleus, as one of a cluster of miracles (18.206). Again, Diomedes says that if need be he will capture Troy with the help of only a single companion (9.48); Achilleus prays for the same thing, as part of a latent death wish (16.97). Sometimes the doublet is outside the poem. Paris shoots an arrow into Diomedes's foot (11.376). This sounds like Achilleus's heel. The shield in *Iliad* 18, so full of sound and motion, is in fact an image of the world disk, encircled by the River Ocean. In the funeral games, we find, unexpectedly, Epeios and his horse, and the archers and the axes. Priam's trip in book 24 is like a descent to the underworld, with the tomb, the river, the sudden darkness, and the escort of Hermes. This use of parallels is all impressive, but it is not clear that it is a criterion of greatness.

What, then, is great literature? Several generations ago, so the story goes, a renowned professor of English at my university spent much of his time reading aloud from the assigned texts. After some passages he would say, "Exquisite!" and after others "Execrable!" These exclamations must have passed for literary criticism in his eyes. Today's more demanding student will not accept unsubstantiated judgments. The truth may not be self-evident, but the teacher is in a position to offer guidance to a fuller awareness.

There are two rules: keep the discussion simple, and keep the interpretations close to the text.

We begin by conceding that there are no infallible rules for great literature. If there were, it could be composed to order. How, then, is it recognized? If we may switch to television, a less demanding medium, students will admit that seeing Olivier as *King Lear* has more effect on them than watching an episode of a soap opera. "Effect"—this is the key. Students must be encouraged to react to what they read and to analyze their reactions. They will respond to greatness in literature by feeling, and perhaps even by physical symptoms. Emily Dickinson said that poetry made her body feel cold (Bianchi 276), and A. E. Housman that it made his skin bristle and his eyes fill with tears (193).

Perhaps, then, great literature can be recognized by emotional tact. Does this mean that rational discussion of the question is unthinkable? Not quite. One of the few critical ideas that students are likely to have picked up in school is the notion that "great literature has the quality of universality." The words they know, but the meaning may have eluded them. We can suggest that universality means providing a thrill of recognition, a sense of familiarity. "A work of the past . . . may treat so directly of what is permanent in the human condition that time can get no hold on it. . . . 'Yes, this is true,' we say of such writing, 'this is how it is' " (Carne-Ross 3).

In the *Iliad* the universality is that of human nature, which has not changed in three thousand years ("As they were so ye are," says Ra in Shaw's *Caesar and Cleopatra*). "With Shakespeare, we are amazed that we already know so much about his characters even before they walk on to the stage" (Levin 34), and the same effect is true of Homer. We recognize them all: Telamonian Aias, dull-witted and inarticulate, the bulwark of the Achaians; the lesser Aias, the venomous little cutthroat, the best at catching and killing men who are running away; Hektor, "the sort of hero that we ourselves, at our moments of greatest aspiration, might hope to be" (Redfield, *Nature* 28); Helen, the self-centered beauty, who even in her weaving glorifies the unhappiness she has caused; Idomeneus, the grizzled imperturbable professional soldier; Nestor, the aged repository of wisdom, like Polonius, but with a glorious past; Odysseus, the consummate diplomat, "the one who survives" (Lattimore, *Iliad* 51); Paris, the spoiled amoral younger brother, who is perfectly willing to do the proper thing if only he knew what it was.

But besides the major figures, a host of lesser characters are called into existence only to be killed, characters etched forever in our memories willy-nilly by some pathetic vignette: Axylos, who entertained all comers in his house by the wayside but whom none of them availed to help; Deukalion, who, with his arm hanging heavy, looked death in the face; Dolon, evil to look on, swift-footed, a single son among five sisters; Euchenor, a seer's son, who chose to fall in battle rather than waste away in a painful sickness; blameless Gorgythion, whose head in death drooped to one side, like a poppy heavy with seed; Polydoros, youngest-born and best-beloved son of Priam, and swiftest of foot; Rhesos, who found reality crueler than his nightmare; Simoeisios, the son of a shepherd girl, cut down like some black poplar in the marsh before he could tend his parents in their old age.

So much is straightforward. On a closer look we see the poet using his characters to manipulate our responses. He chooses to tell of the parting of Hektor and Andromache, and he chooses to include in it a picture of the basic family: the beautiful bride, younger surely than her years, who has lost everyone but her husband, whose doom she foresees; the young man who knows the city will fall and his wife will belong to another but who is ashamed not to go out and get killed; the helpless infant who is not used to seeing daddy in his working clothes. None of this is essential to the story; it is included primarily to stir our emotions.

We naturally expect to think well of the Greek general. Yet Agamemnon at his first appearance acts against the will of his army, threatens a priest, and tells a father that his daughter is a sex object. All this occurs in the first fifty lines. As the poem proceeds, three times he tells the army to abandon the siege. When his brother is wounded, he shudders—not so much from fraternal concern as from the humiliation he will incur if Helen is left in Trojan hands. He needs the perquisites of office and demands immediate recompense for Chryseis. In promising a reward to Teukros, he says, "First after myself, I will put into your hands some great gift" (8.289). He is convinced that he was within his rights in taking Briseis and cannot see Achilleus's viewpoint ("Let him yield . . ." 9.160). The poet molds our attitude to the supreme commander, and thereby colors our reaction to Agamemnon's mode of warfare. Vicious in battle, he mutilates his victims and violates convention by killing suppliants (6.63, 11.143). He is repeatedly compared to a remorseless lion and wades through slaughter until his hands are spattered with bloody filth (11.169).

There are other surprises in store for us. Patroklos, it seems, is Achilleus's menial. In book 1, he is told to bring out the girl and hand her over to the heralds. In book 9 he is told to mix drinks for the visitors. In book 11 he is told to go out and see what is going on. Then, suddenly, Nestor addresses him as an adviser and special friend of Achilleus; Patroklos is invited to assume Achilleus's armor and play his role and, in fact, becomes Achilleus's double. When Patroklos is killed, it is Achilleus that lies as one dead, surrounded by mourners and supported by his mother in a pietà tableau. On Patroklos's death something gentle goes out of Achilleus, and he becomes a killing machine (Whitman 181).

And what of Achilleus himself? Well, he is clearly the protagonist, the hero of the poem. He is great and grand and chilly and remote. We can admire him, but we cannot love him. When he fights Hektor, there is no doubt where our sympathies lie. Later, when the Greeks stand around the dead Hektor and stab him and when Achilleus drags him behind his chariot, their actions are utterly repellent. By this time the ruin of Achilleus is complete. He has lost the one person he cared for. He was once chivalrous, but now he has turned his back on the heroic ideal and kills suppliants (20.471, 21.117). His whole battlefield performance is brutal. His very chariot is splashed with blood, and his hands are spattered with bloody filth (20.503). In other words, he is just like Agamemnon. How could he suffer any worse fate? In the last two books he regains his humanity and is perhaps redeemed in our eyes, but it is too late.

We sometimes hear it said that the *Iliad* is incomplete, because it does not show Achilleus's death. Are we then to see the poem as simply a magnificent fragment? Achilleus and his mother know he is short-lived. After the death of Patroklos he wishes for immediate death, becomes indifferent to worldly possessions and to human food, is sustained by ambrosia (a preservative for corpses), and admits that he is fated to die at Troy. His mother has told him that his death will follow hard upon that of Hektor, his horse has broken into speech and warned him of his impending fate, and the dying Hektor has foreseen the circumstances. Achilleus has devoted himself to death by committing a lock of his hair to Patroklos and has given orders for his own burial. He looks forward to his death with resignation, almost with relief. His work on earth is done. What more could the poet do? The death of Achilleus (like the fall of Troy) is inevitable, and close, by the end of the poem.

In short, with little effort we can recognize the players in the drama and understand what makes them do the things they do. That is one reason why the poem is so moving. There is another, perhaps related. The *Iliad* represents the wrath of Achilleus: its cause, its course, its effect. The poem is serious, it is substantial, it is complete; the language is literary and somewhat ornate; the action is for the most part portrayed directly rather than narrated. The poem arouses our pity and fear. It has unity of plot. It is the story of a man of great repute and good fortune, who suffers terrible misfortune through some wrong action on his part. That is, anachronism or not, it fits Aristotle's definition of tragedy.

The *Odyssey* is a very different poem. It does not deal with great psychological issues, and it lacks the tragic aura of the *Iliad*. One is not tempted to weep over it. "The best works of imagination are those which draw most tears," said Voltaire. Tragedy is a "greater" genre than comedy, and to this extent the *Odyssey* is lesser than the *Iliad*.

Nevertheless it is entertaining and accessible. Even though the characters are shallow, or at least "opaque" and "inscrutable" (Griffin, *Homer on Life* 76), the adventure story of the king who reestablishes himself on his throne strikes a responsive chord. In fact, if we are to find "universality" in the *Odyssey*, we should seek it not so much in the realistic portrayal of human nature as in the pervasive influence of *Märchen*. The poem has dozens of episodes that we recognize from the fairy tales of our childhood. Since the point is essential for our argument, it is worth our while to catalog them at length, pausing only to cite *comparanda*: the homecoming husband (Aarne and Thompson 974); the bear's son (Carpenter 136); the son avenges his father (Thompson P233.6); playing for time (Woodhouse 219); the bride must sew a garment for the groom's father (Thompson H383.2.3); a drink causes magic forgetfulness (Thompson D1365.2); a man disguises himself as an animal (Thompson K1823); a wizard undergoes successive transformations (Thompson D610); Venusberg (Thompson F131.1); a man has a fairy wife for seven years (Thompson F302.10); the fairy mistress surrenders a man to his mortal wife (Thompson F302.5.1); the husband outwits his adulterous wife and her paramour (Aarne and Thompson 1359); recognition by a person's tears at the recital of his own exploits (Thompson H14.2); a voyage to an earthly paradise (Thompson F111); enchantment by eating fairy food (Page, *Folktales* 14); the ogre blinded (Aarne and Thompson 1137); the captor beguiled by an equivocal name (Thompson K602); escape from death under a ram's belly (Thompson K603); the taboo against looking into a bag of winds (Thompson C322.1); the ogre and his wife (Page, *Folktales* 28); a sorceress transforms men into animals (Page, *Folktales* 57); a magic object keeps off enchantment (Thompson D1578); a journey to the lower world (Thompson F80); a summoned dead man prophesies (Thompson M301.14); unremitting torture as punishment (Thompson Q501); the Lorelei and her magic song (Page, *Folktales* 87); ears stopped with wax to avoid an enchanting song (Thompson J672.1); the slaughter of the sacred cattle (Page, *Folktales* 82); death by drowning for breaking a prohibition (Thompson C923); transportation during a magic sleep (Thompson D1976.1); the ship turned to stone (Thompson D471.3); the stolen prince (Woodhouse 229); the disguised man recognized by a dog (Thompson H173); the husband returns in humble disguise (Thompson K1815); recognition by a scar (Thompson H51); the husband arrives home just as his wife is about to marry another (Thompson N681); the suitors' contest (Thompson H331); recognition by the unique ability to bend a bow (Thompson H31.2); the archery competition (Germain 11); recognition by describing a unique bed (Thompson H16.4); identity tested by recounting shared experiences (Thompson H15); the ascending scale of affection in which the father stands higher than the wife (Kakridis, *Homeric* 156). With so many familiar motifs, it is small wonder if we find the poem congenial.

Several of these motifs occur more than once in the poem, and we see the same love of parallelism that we encountered in the *Iliad*. We are constantly reminded of the similarities between Agamemnon and Odysseus. A stranger at the gate is welcomed repeatedly, and this hospitality seems like a fact of life, rather than a motif, until we see it violated by the Cyclops. Odysseus tells a lying version of his adventures five times. He is recognized at home seven times. Sometimes the final iteration is climactic, and so we have anticipatory doublets. Four times Odysseus arrives in a city in disguise and is offered or given a bath by a woman; four times blood is shed at the banquet (Clarke, *Art* 54, 16). Even the characters are doubled. We have two hospitable goddesses (Kalypso, Circe), two faithful herdsmen (Eumaios, Philoitios), two aged nurses (Eurykleia, Eurynome; see Fenik, *Studies* 172).

The universality that provides a thrill of recognition, realistic and moving characterization, tales so old they are a part of our folk memory, story-telling skills that use repetition to good effect—all these contribute to Homer's greatness. But, in the end, to read Homer is more important than to talk about him. No matter which poem is assigned, the students should read it complete—if not in Greek, at any rate in English. The poet composed more than the favorite anthologized bits, and it is only by dealing with the poem as an artistic whole that we can hope to recover something of the effect he intended. In the classroom, if we are fond of Homer, we are obliged to convey something of our enthusiasm and to show that it is not a blind prejudice. Not without reason has the tale of Troy fulfilled Helen's prophecy,

> Wide shall it spread, and last through ages long,
> Example sad! and theme of future song.
> (Pope, *Il.* 6.357–58)

On Recovering Homer

Robert Zaslavsky

We must beware, even when reading modern texts, of being the moderns whom Hegel so aptly distinguished from the ancients. The moderns, he said, have a tendency to come to things with the concept ready-made, while the ancients approached things with a natural consciousness that, "testing itself against every separate part . . . and philosophizing about everything . . . made itself . . . active through and through" (52). So, instead of leading phenomena a merry chase, we must be led by them; instead of adopting an Achillean intransigence, we must enact an Odyssean wandering. In other words, we must abjure a frozen fame (*kleos*) and navigate a heartsore home-coming (*nostos*).

We must understand, then, that just as the reader's task is to understand a text in its own terms first, so too the teacher's task is to present the text in its own terms first. That is, we as teachers must first hear the text speak to us in its own language, and then we must make it speak through us to our students. This procedure is difficult enough when the text is in a con-temporary tongue; the difficulty is greater when the text is in an alien tongue and still greater if the alien tongue is noncontemporary. Since students usually perceive Homer through the filter of translation, a filter that admits of degrees of opacity, our responsibility is to ensure that as little as possible is filtered out. That such a responsibility can be fulfilled is shown by Thomas Aquinas, who, using William of Moerbeke's Latin translations, wrote astute commentaries on Aristotle, even though he himself knew no Greek. And since Homer is no less a philosopher than a poet, as Plato and Aristotle well knew, one should be able to gain reasonable access to his works through adequate, if not perfect, translation.

The question of what constitutes an adequate translation must be an-swered, in our own minds at least, before we enter the classroom. Our answer can be based on critical evaluations of various translations or on our own knowledge of ancient Greek. But we can also thematize the issue of translation in the classroom as a way of penetrating the work itself. This approach alerts students to the problem of translation as a propaedeutic to the use, an immunization to the lures, of any particular translation, even the "best." It also sets up a dialectic of translational biases through which the work may be allowed to begin to emerge in its own right. In this way, we can develop an antidote to the contempt bred both by the intimacy of an overly loose translation and by the remoteness of an overly literal trans-lation (although the latter seems preferable to the former). We can accomplish this in practice by distributing at the outset a small section of text in a variety of translations. I have always used the opening passage of the *nekyia* of *Odyssey* 11, for the trivial reason that it enables me to use the brilliant if quirky abridged translation of the passage—employing Anglo-Saxon versification techniques—that opens Ezra Pound's first canto, and for the more serious reason that it raises, quickly and disturbingly, certain key theological issues. I also require that the students write a paper on a manageably small section of the text using at least two translations.

The point of this exercise is to encourage students to leave behind unexamined assumptions in their reading of Homer. But this can be done in other ways as well. For example, if we simply take the title *Iliad* and compare it to the announced theme of the invocation, we are immediately led to ask what is indeed part of the first question that Porphyry articulates and answers in his *Homeric Questions*:

> Since Achilleus was generally the best, we must ask why the poet did not title the *Iliad* the *Achilleid*. And we would reply that since the account in the Odyssey was composed around only one hero, the title is quite apt. In the *Iliad*, on the other hand, even if Achilleus was more the best than anyone else, still the others also seem to be among the best. For the poet's design makes it clear that not only was Achilleus heroic but so also were almost all the others. . . . Therefore, since the poet could not possibly have aptly titled it from one person alone, he titled it from the city, and Achilleus is thus allowed to emerge organically within this setting as the best of the best.   (A.1; trans. mine. Cf. Benardete, "Achilles" 1)

The trilogy of modern works that explore this view of the *Iliad* should form the basis of any reader's consideration of that poem: Cedric H. Whitman's *Homer and the Heroic Tradition*, which explores Homer's "intellectual or intuitive penetration of the themes and character shapes which constitute the heroic typology" of "a totally conceived heroic world" (155, 123); Gregory Nagy's *Best of the Achaeans*, an impressive extended philological anthropological appendix to Whitman; and James M. Redfield's *Nature and Culture in the* Iliad, a more philosophically grounded revision and reorientation of Whitman's analysis, in which Hektor is given his rightful place alongside Achilleus. Redfield argues that the question of intention—which Whitman sees as authorial (114; cf. 10, 93, 125, 153, 154, 165, 243, 250, 255) and Nagy sees as traditional (3; cf. 4–5, 20–21)—is really the question of meaning:

> The characters in a poem are as the poet made them, and he made them as he would have them for the needs of his work. . . . We ask

what sort of meaning the poet is conveying and how he seeks to convey it; we shall find this meaning conveyed [only] in the poem as a whole. We thus shift our interest from character to plot, taking "plot" . . . as that implicit conceptual unity which has given the work its actual form. We investigate the meaning of the work. . . . (Redfield 23; cf. x–xi, xiii)

Clearly, we must take seriously our experience of the Homeric poems, of their conceptual unity, an experience that was certainly shared by the earliest readers of the poems from whom we have written testimony. If we do, the pedantic drive to anatomize the poems becomes senseless (except insofar as it collects suggestive and useful data for the unitarian quest for meaning), and the unitarian assumption is seen to be methodologically unassailable:

Stories . . . dramatize values; each story is a kind of thought-experiment which explores the problematic of a culture. As the culture is complex it gives rise to many heroes and many stories. From this point of view the *Iliad* and the *Odyssey* . . . can be thought of as essentially contemporary. These poems elaborate contrasting perspectives on a common set of problems. (Redfield 219)

The Homeric poems, then, delineate heroes in the world and the world of heroes. And if the *Iliad* presents us with the range of soul types that constitute the culture-cultic hero, then the *Odyssey* presents us with the nature hero. (Indeed, the first appearance of the word nature [*physis*] in extant Greek literature is in the *Odyssey* 10.303, in the accusative, the only occurrence of the word in Homer.) So instead of seeing the *Iliad* as the expression of the heroic world *simpliciter* and the *Odyssey* as the expression of the post- or extraheroic world, we should see the two poems together as an expression of the heroic view in all its dimensions, as Socrates suggests in the *Cratylus* 398c6–e3 (trans. mine):

HERMOGENES. What about *hero* [*heros*]?
SOCRATES. That's not too hard to see, and since the word is only slightly altered, its origin out of *love* [*eros*] is clear.
HERMOGENES. How do you mean that?
SOCRATES. Don't you see that heroes are half gods?
HERMOGENES. So?
SOCRATES. Presumably all heroes are born from the love act of a god with a mortal female or a goddess with a mortal male. And if you also think of ancient Attic sounds, you will see more clearly that from the word *love* [*eros*], the word for the act from which the

heroes were born, there has been only a slight alteration. And this is one possible explanation of the word *heroes*. Another possible explanation is that they were named *heroes* because they were wise and formidable orators who were adept in conversation and hence in questioning [*erotan*]. And *speaking* [*legein*] is "*saying*" [*eirein*]. Therefore, as we just said, in Attic sounding, the heroes are said to be those orators who are adept in questioning [*erotetikoi*], and so the heroic clan turns out to be the race of orators and sophists.

The "erotic" heroes are the heroes of the *Iliad*, whose plot is motivated by three loves (the love of Helen, the love of fame, and the love of Patroklos: see Benardete, "Aristeia" 21–24); the "erotetic" heroes are the heroes of the *Odyssey*, Odysseus and his nearest and dearest, whose actions are motivated by every degree of questioning, from simple informational inquiry to refined existential skepticism. It is fitting, then, that the patron gods, as it were, of the *Iliad* are Ares (manly courage: see *Cratylus* 407c9–d5) and Aphrodite (foam-born love) and of the *Odyssey* Hermes (speech: see *Cratylus* 407e1–408b7) and Athene (intellect: see *Cratylus* 407a5–c2). And although no one would need to defend the singling out of Hermes and Athene for the *Odyssey*, one might need to defend the singling out of Ares and Aphrodite for the *Iliad* by pointing out that they are the only two gods wounded (in Diomedes's *aristeia*, *Il.* 5.165–417, 846–906) and that the description of their conjoint predicament at *Odyssey* 8.266–369 is a particularly telling commentary on the *Iliad*. Contraposed to these pairs of patron gods are the respective troublemaker gods; in the *Iliad* it is Hera (the airy lovable one: see *Cratylus* 404b9–c4) and in the *Odyssey* Poseidon (the shrewd shuffling shaker: see *Cratylus* 402d7–403a2).

The two poems also differ in the aspects of the traditional Greek tetrad of virtues that they isolate for treatment. In the *Iliad*, the focus is on courage and justice, and hence on eros as, on the one hand, a cause of strife (*eris*, in which the omega is displaced by the iota of mobile slipperiness: see *Cratylus* 426e6–427a1) and as, on the other, a motivator toward fame (see *Symposium* 208b7–209e4). And since courage and justice are associated with *thymos* (spirit), the *Iliad* focuses on agonistics and war, on the lion (*the* thymoeidetic beast: see *Republic* 9.588b1–92b6; see also Hartigan) and the horse (see Geddes 205–18, 229–32, 341–43), on the straight line as the paradigmatic vector of action (the Doloneia being the exception that proves the rule), on disguise as fatal (as shown by Patroklos's, and ultimately Hektor's, doom), on self-assertion and righteous indignation, on daylight and plains (see Flaumenhaft), in a word on the narrowly political and legalistic.

In the *Odyssey*, by contrast, the focus is on wisdom and moderation, and hence on eros as a pleasant natural indulgence, on the one hand, and as a sacramental communion, on the other. And since wisdom and moderation are associated with calculation (*to logistikon*), the *Odyssey* focuses ultimately on peace, on the dog (the beast with a philosophical nature: see *Republic* 2.375d10–76b7; see also Geddes 218–28, 232–35), on the serpentine line as the paradigmatic vector of action, on disguise as a curative device, on subtlety and deception, on self-abnegation and moral expansiveness, on darkness and caves (see Flaumenhaft), in a word on the broadly philosophical and poetic.

It is consistent with this difference between the two poems that the pains (*alge'*) mentioned in the invocation to the *Iliad* are brought down by Achilleus on an entire people, his own, and in this way he lives up to his name (see Nagy 69–72, 74–75); while the pains (*algea*) mentioned in the invocation to the *Odyssey* are suffered by no one but No One, Odysseus himself (see *Odyssey* 9.366–67). It is further consistent that in the *Iliad* Homer maintains strict authorial neutrality to such an extent that it cannot be said which of the heroes he favors, while in the *Odyssey* his partisanship for Odysseus is manifest from the start (see Clay, "Beginning").

Clearly, then, the themes and motifs of the Homeric poems are not completely alien to us, and yet they are not completely familiar to us either. And this has been the situation for all readers of the poems since they were first written down, the difference between us and the first readers being a difference in degree rather than a difference in kind. But the difference in degree must not be minimized. The Homeric poems are exotic, and their exoticism consists in their presentation of a culture model that is no longer ours. And if the battle milieu of the *Iliad* is not excessively more alien to us than the whaling milieu of Melville's *Moby-Dick*, or if the theology of the poems is not excessively more alien to us than the theology of Milton's *Paradise Lost*, the point is less that our habitual modes of thought are near to Homer than that they are far even from our more immediate literary-cultural heritage. For most of us cannot see the *Iliad* in Faulkner's *Fable* (whose setting, theme, and rhetoric are deliberately and effectively Homeric, with the substitution of the Christian theology for the Greek) or the *Odyssey* in Hawthorne's *Scarlet Letter* (whose 24 chapters mirror the 24 traditional books of the *Odyssey*—perhaps nowhere more tellingly than in the eleventh chapter, where the Homeric *nekyia* becomes "the interior of a heart"—and whose characters are dark American versions of the personae of the *Odyssey*, with Chillingworth as the wandering Odysseus, Hester as the fiber-artisan Penelope, Dimmesdale as the suitors, and Pearl as Telemachos). And we do not see the *Iliad* and the *Odyssey* in these works, because we do not see them in themselves. On the one hand, our loss of intimacy with the Homeric works blinds us to their subliminal presence in the works modeled on them;

on the other hand, the subliminal presence of the Homeric works in the later works promotes in us a tendency to see the earlier works through the later versions of them instead of the other way around. The result is that we ignore the organic relation between the earlier and later works in favor either of understanding the ancient works through modern categories or of ravaging the ancient works in order to convert them into grist for the source mill.

The difficulty is to preserve the exoticism of the Homeric poems, to show that their appeal is grounded in that exoticism, to understand them instead of making them understand us:

> We understand Homer's meaning only when we interpret him in relation to the whole system of potential meanings he presumes. Thus is defined for us . . . the task of translation; we must know the culture in order to interpret the story, just as we must know the language to translate the text.
>
> On the other hand, we are translating from a dead language. We cannot interview the Homeric Greeks and elicit new data. The poem does not protest against misinterpretation. . . . Homeric culture, further, is transmitted to us only in poetic imitation. We should not speak of the "background" of the poems, as though we could reconstruct Homeric society and then apply this reconstruction to interpretation of the poems. On the contrary: we discover the society by interpreting the poems, just as we learn Homeric Greek, not in order to read Homer, but by reading Homer.   (Redfield, *Nature* x–xi)

This is an eloquent and compelling manifesto, although Redfield would have made the paradox clearer if he had said that we learn Homeric Greek in order to read Homer only by reading Homer. And if this is a circle, then one should realize that in escaping the circle one pays the price of losing the circle's integrity, that only by reflectively living the circle do we see and experience the circle as true and integral. The difficulties of such an enterprise are enormous, but the rewards are the greater for that.

Let us end, then, as the Platonic Socrates and Aristotle end when they are about to continue a discussion beyond its apparent end, by saying with them, πάλιν αρχώμεθα 'let us begin again.'

Focusing on Homeric Values

J. Frank Papovich

"With blood and muck all spattered upon him," Hektor leaves the battle raging on the plains of Troy and returns to the city, where he finds Andromache with their infant son at her breast. Together they speak of the horrors of war and the harsh specter of her enslavement by an Achaian warrior. Hektor reaches out to his son, who shrinks in fright from his dreadfully armed father. Then, in what seems a momentary respite from the terror of their world, Hektor removes his plume-crested helmet, tenderly jostles his now quieted son on his armed breast, and prays to the Olympians:

> Zeus, and you other immortals, grant that this
>   boy, who is my son,
> may be as I am, pre-eminent among the
>   Trojans,
> great in strength, as I am, and rule strongly over
>   Ilion;
> and some day let them say of him: "He is better
>   by far than his father,"
> as he comes in from the fighting; and let him kill
>   his enemy
> and bring home the bloodied spoils, and delight
>   the heart of his mother.
>   (*Il.* 6.476–81; trans. Lattimore)[1]

Coming on this scene, many of our students may be disturbed by Hektor's prayer. After all, they reason, should not such a father, troubled by the thought of his wife's grief, wish that his son be spared the agony of war and pray instead for a life of peace?

As contradictory as this prayer may seem, other passages are still more difficult to resolve. Throughout the *Odyssey*, for example, students come to sympathize more and more with Odysseus. Overcoming every obstacle of men and gods, he longs only to return to the land of his father, his home, and his wife and son. Yet the relief and joy that many students feel on Odysseus's return often vanish as his "bloodthirsty" vengeance unravels. If our students see the climax of the *Odyssey* as an unjustified slaughter of the suitors, who often seem, in Lattimore's words, "more an intolerable nuisance than an actual menace" (Odyssey *of Homer* 17), we may be forced to allude to "the way things were" or to apologize for the "barbaric" excesses of our once honorable hero. But by doing so, we risk leaving students with a bitter aftertaste of what may be their first and last sampling of ancient Greek literature.

Before we accept such a situation, we should make every effort to help students understand not only the texts before them but also the cultural context that gave rise to such texts. This endeavor is especially important in teaching the Homeric texts, which, as oral narratives, are far more indebted to the traditions of their culture than are most literary narratives.[2] Yet the need to inform ourselves of the cultural context of the Homeric poems is often unrecognized. We are lulled into a false confidence by our perspective on the ancient Greeks and their traditions. So much of their culture stands as a source of our own that we often assume that these Greeks must have judged people and reacted to events as we do. We need, however, to set aside our familiar perceptual patterns and the misleading assumptions they generate. For if we fail to understand the original intentions in the Greek text, we may fail, in large part, to understand the text at all.

We can help our students better understand Homeric values by examining selected words from the original Greek texts. A rudimentary familiarity with the concerns of Homeric society, combined with close study of the range of key Greek value words in the texts, enables students to see beyond the patterns of their own culture and begin to understand the culture that informs the actions of the Homeric characters.

As an aid to our study of key Greek value words, lexicons are of limited help. By dividing up words, particularly value words with abstract connotations, into different "meanings," lexicons may fail to communicate why such words behave as they do. Consider, for example, the word *arete*, which has the various meanings of "goodness, excellence, prowess, success, prosperity, strength." It is more useful to think of value words as having a range of usage rather than many different meanings of which we must choose only one. Lexicons offer us the remnants of once coherent, though alien, values or concepts that have been fragmented by our own culturally bound perception. When this fragmentation occurs with words that are central to the major themes of a text, misinterpretation can result.

For readers who do not know Greek, thinking of key terms in the original Greek may seem impossible. But A. W. H. Adkins suggests a way of circumventing this difficulty by transliterating rather than translating such terms. If students read central passages where such terms have been transliterated and spend one or two class sessions discussing the range of usage of those terms in various contexts, they will jump to fewer unjustified conclusions and miss fewer meaningful connections.[3]

As Adkins points out, value words have both a "descriptive" and an "evaluative" usage.[4] They describe certain characteristics and either approve or disapprove of the possession of those characteristics. When we translate *arete* as "good," we can assume that the evaluative meanings of the Greek and English are nearly the same—both words approve of the thing to which they are applied. Yet the qualities that determine "goodness" in things of the same kind may not be the same in Greek as in English. For example, the quality that most often characterized a man with *arete* was his success alone, with the means of his success counting for little or nothing. But in our culture, these means may indeed be more important in determining a person's goodness than the simple fact of success.

To discover what qualities were most important to Homeric man, we need to make one further distinction in evaluation. As Adkins observes, in any society value words may be divided into two broad groups. The first, which he terms "competitive," refers to evaluations made on the basis of success or failure, with success ranked highest. Intentions are of no importance. We would not commend a general by saying he was a good commander but never won any battles. Success in war is paramount; intentions matter little, for no one intends to fail. Intentions do matter, however, with the second group of value words, which refer to cooperative activities. In cooperative arrangements, such as contracts or alliances, justice and fairness are of primary importance, and questions about intentions are appropriate. We might well want to know if a general is a good ally. Before deciding, we might ask if in his attempt to win a battle he intended to sacrifice the troops of his allies.

As students will discover in studying the conflicts between Achilleus and Agamemnon and between Odysseus and the suitors, the competitive values were more highly regarded than the cooperative. For in Homeric society, the balance between existence and annihilation was precarious. Cooperative virtues were valued, but in times of crisis, which were frequent, the pre-eminence of the competitive qualities and of the success they imparted became unmistakable. With such a scale of values, disputes between chiefs who were sufficiently angry to refuse arbitration could not be settled by referring to the "higher" virtues of cooperation, even in joint military expeditions. Further, since there was no authority higher than each individual chief and since concession to informal arbitration might have been regarded as a sign of weakness or failure, the seeds of dispute were inherent in the system (Adkins, "Homeric Values" 10). Indeed, the main plots of both the Homeric poems reflect what occurs when such competition progresses from an abstract value to concrete action.

Since the conditions of Homeric society largely determine the range of key value words, I find it necessary to present briefly to my students the relation between society and lexical usage before they can analyze the poems in terms appropriate to the Homeric context. To make this cultural infor-

mation readily accessible, I here summarize relevant material more exten-
sively discussed by M. I. Finley and A. W. H. Adkins (see Works Cited).
I find, however, that providing students with such historical information
does not require lengthy lectures. Just as cultural background and dramatic
foreground are nearly indistinguishable in the view of an audience in a
traditional oral performance (where preserving and transmitting customs and
values are a central aim), so this material can be presented to students as
part of their initial experience in reading and discussing the poems. In class,
I begin with my own brief explanations of various cultural conditions and
have students supplement these explanations by analyzing, either in small
group discussions or in short written assignments, select passages with key
words transliterated rather than translated. Below, I use examples of such
passages to illustrate the points of my discussion.

The social organization and value system of the Homeric poems are based
firmly on the *oikos*, or the noble household, which was the highest form of
political and economic as well as social organization. The *oikoi* were spread
across the countryside with no other governing institutions to promote their
growth and well-being or to prevent their complete annihilation. Some sense
of community undeniably existed in Homeric society, but in a crisis, or
whenever the aims of the *oikos* diverged from those of the wider community,
the claims of the *oikos* were always primary.

Command of each *oikos* was the responsibility of the local warrior-chieftain,
who was both denoted and commended by the synonymous adjectives *agathos*
and *esthlos*. Given the autonomy of the *oikos* and the absence of any higher
authority, preserving the *oikos* clearly required the martial abilities of the
agathos, whose qualities were denoted and commended by the noun *arete*
(superlative adjective form: *aristos*). *Arete* was the power or ability to succeed
in some action, and the highest use of *arete* commended the successful
warrior, the *agathos*. To help students discover this emphasis on success in
war, I ask them to consider the following short passage, an address of the
Lykian Sarpedon to his comrade Glaukos:

> Glaukos, why is it you and I are *timan*, honoured,
>   before others
> with pride of place, the choice meats and the
>   filled wine cups
> in Lykia, and all men look on us as if we were
>   immortals,
> and we are appointed a great piece of land by the
>   banks of Xanthos,
> good land, orchard and vineyard, and ploughland
>   for the planting of wheat?

> Therefore it is our duty in the forefront of the
>   Lykians
> to take our stand, and bear our part of the
>   blazing of battle,
> so that a man of the close-armoured Lykians may
>   say of us:
> "Indeed, these are no ignoble men who are lords
>   of Lykia,
> these kings of ours, who feed upon the fat sheep
>   appointed
> and drink the exquisite sweet wine, since indeed
>   there is *esthlos*, strength
> of valour, in them. . . ."   (*Il.* 12.310–21)

With only two key words transliterated, my students can better see the values that motivate these warriors to join gladly "in the blazing of battle." Sarpedon and Glaukos deserve the position of *agathos* because they fight in the first ranks, and there they either succeed and win honor or die and bring honor to their opponent. What becomes clear, then, is that the *agathoi*, originally a response to warlike conditions, came to value and even need war as a means of maintaining privileged status. A brutal necessity, war grew to have a positive value for the *agathoi*. And so Hektor's puzzling wish for his son's happiness in a life of war and bloodied spoils becomes much easier for our students both to understand and to justify. If Astyanax, son of Hektor and Andromache, were to lead the best of lives, war was necessary.

Another important concept closely associated with *arete* is *time*. *Time* is usually rendered "honor," "compensation," or "penalty"—a combination, as we see it, of dissimilar elements. Verb forms are *tinein* and *timan*, rendered "to honor"; (*apo*) *tinein*, "to pay a price"; and (*apo*)*tinesthai*, "to punish." While often denoting and chiefly acquired by the possession of material goods, *time* is not equivalent to such goods. A man's *time* is his position on a scale that ranks gods at the top and the homeless beggar, such as the disguised Odysseus on his return to Ithaka, at the bottom. To honor (*timan*) a man is to move him away from the position of defenseless beggar. To dishonor (*atiman*) a man is to do the reverse. Thus *time* denotes and commends all that distinguishes the life of a prosperous *agathos* from that of a beggar—property, rights, and status.

Time was not an absolute quality but, rather, a relative quality (available in limited quantity). *Time* awarded to one man must be *time* withdrawn from another. To get back *time* is *tinesthai*, "to punish." But translating *tinesthai* "to punish" is not always appropriate. While the sack of Troy was *tinesthai* in the sense of "to punish," that punishment also and more fundamentally involved getting back *time* in the form of Helen, the goods stolen from Menelaos by Paris, the stripped armor of the Trojan warriors, and the booty acquired in the general looting of the city. If, in this case, translating *tinesthai* "to punish" makes students miss important connotations concerning the restoration of *time*, such a translation in other passages may make them miss the basic sense. When Alkinoös proposes to make a collection among the Phaiakians and *tinesthai*, he is suggesting not that his counselors should punish the people but, rather, that they should replenish their *time* that has been depleted by giving friendship gifts to Odysseus (13.13–15). These two separate incidents, which at first seem to students only peripherally related, were closely related to the Homeric Greeks because of the importance of *time*.

While each *agathos* was well prepared to defend his *time* and *oikos*, no *agathos* could depend on himself alone. And since human beings in Homeric society had no rights except those they could defend by force or have guaranteed by being members of an *oikos*, the family, retainers, and servants of the *agathos* who depended on his *time* in the form of food, clothing, shelter, and status could, in turn, be depended on by the *agathos*. The *agathos* and his dependents, thus constituting a tightly bound support system, were distinguished from the rest of the world by the word *philos*.

The *agathos* traveling away from his *oikos* presented a special problem, for outside the *oikos* there was no real central institution to protect the rights, much less the existence, of the traveler. The traveler must supplicate an *agathos* who headed an *oikos* and hope to be received as a *philos*. Such a dependent relationship between a traveler and an *agathos* was a type of *philos* relation denoted by the word *xeinos*, usually rendered guest-friend (*xeinos* can denote both guest and friend). Thus the stranger who had a *xeinos* had an effective substitute for a kinsman, a substitute who would defend his guest-friend as he would any other member of his *oikos* and who would react to a loss of *time* by his *xeinos* as a loss of his own *time*. The *agathos* who agreed to receive a suppliant had, in turn, imposed a similar set of obligations on the received traveler, in effect guaranteeing his own *time* should he ever travel to the homeland of his *xeinos*. (This explains why *xeinos* has the dual denotation of guest and host, for by accepting the rights of a guest, an *agathos* also accepts the responsibility of a host should the occasion arise.) These reciprocal obligations were typically observed by the exchange of *xeinos* gifts, denoted by the word *xeineia*. Never were such gifts given by a host without proper recompense, whether immediate or years away, to self or kin.

The meeting of the Lykian Glaukos and the Greek Diomedes provides an excellent example for students to see the power of the *xeinos* relationship. The two have met in the heat of battle, and Diomedes has asked who his opponent is. After detailing his Lykian ancestors, Glaukos is interrupted by a "gladdened" Diomedes:

> [Diomedes] drove his spear deep into the
>   prospering earth, and in winning
> words of friendliness he spoke to the shepherd of
>   the people:
> "See now, you are my *xeinos*, guest-friend, from
>   far in the time of our fathers.
> Brilliant Oineus once was *xeinos*, host, to
>   Bellerophontes
> the blameless, in his halls, and twenty days he
>   detained him,
> and these two gave to each other fine *xeineia*,
>   gifts in token of friendship.
>
> .   .   .   .
>
>   Therefore I am your *xeinos*,
>   friend and host, in the heart of Argos;
> you are mine in Lykia, when I come to your
>   country.
> Let us avoid each other's spears, even in close
>   fighting.
>
> .   .   .   .
>
> But let us exchange our armour, so that these
>   others may know
> how we claim to be *xeinoi*, guests and friends,
>   from the days of our fathers."   (*Il.* 6.214–31)

Without understanding the situation of the traveler in Homeric society and the workings of the *xeinos* relationship, students usually view this exchange as little more than a quaint aberration in the mechanics of Homeric warfare. But having gained even slight familiarity with Homeric culture, students can see the sense of this pause in battle. While neither Glaukos nor Diomedes have seen or perhaps even heard of each other before, they are *philos* and *xeinos* to each other because of their grandfathers' *xeinos* relationship. Such *xeinos* bonds, furnishing Homeric society with what little stability it possessed, could not be canceled by something so fleeting as a ten-year war between "countries." Diomedes is more closely bound to Glaukos than he is to those Achaians who are not *philos* or *xeinos* to him.

The vengeance of Odysseus, so apparently excessive if students judge by modern-day standards, becomes easier to understand and to justify in the light of such elementary knowledge of Homeric values. Students can weigh the seriousness of the suitors' crimes against Odysseus by noting his yearning for return. He bases his desire for homecoming not simply on his love for Penelope or his longing to see his now grown son, Telemachos (strong as such emotions may be), but more fundamentally on his desire to return to *oikos* and *philoi*. As Odysseus himself claims in refusing Kalypso's invitation: "But even so, what I want and all my days I pine for / is to go back to my *oikos*, house, and see my day of homecoming" (5.219–20). That this should be Odysseus's response wholly befits a man in a society where the necessities of self-preservation and satisfaction are inextricably bound up within the *oikos*. Students can perceive the suitors' offenses as threats to Odysseus's *oikos* and to the continued existence of himself and his *philoi*. Along with the accompanying loss of *time*, such a threat, most obvious in the squandering of the food and wine of the *oikos* and in the open abuse of Telemachos and Penelope, demands a response from Odysseus.

Alerted to the importance of *time* and the *xeinos* relationship, students can understand why the suitors' repeated insults to suppliants aggravate the seriousness of their crimes and justify the vengeance of Odysseus. For not only has his food been wasted in his absence, but when he appears at his own hearth to beg for what is rightfully his, it is denied him by men who squander it before his eyes.

The suitors' mockery of Odysseus's supplications only increases the depravity of their offenses. Antinoös, who throws a footstool at the disguised Odysseus when he asks for a gift of food (17.415–80), will be, in the minds of students aware of these notions of hospitality, doubly deserving of death at Odysseus's hands. For not only does Antinoös trample on the rights of the suppliant Odysseus, but he also fails to fulfill his duties as *xeinos* to Odysseus, since Odysseus had once received Antinoös's father as *xeinos* on Ithaka (this previous relationship also adds an appropriate irony to Odysseus's address to Antinoös as *philos* [17.415]). Ktesippos adds to this fatal offense by proposing a *xeineia*, "guest-gift," for Odysseus and then throwing an ox hoof at him (20.296–300). The last such grievous insult comes from an anonymous suitor who suggests putting "these *xeinoi*, guests [Odysseus and Theoklymenos] in a vessel with many oarlocks / and tak[ing] them to the Sicilians" as slaves, for "there they would fetch a good price" (20.382–83). Given the following transliterated passage, students can observe that Odysseus himself explains his vengeance in precisely such terms:

> These were destroyed by the doom of the gods
>   and their own hard actions,
> for these men paid no *tinein*, attention, at all
>   to any man on earth
> who came their way, no matter if he were
>   base or *esthlos*, noble.   (22.413–15)

By cataloging the suitors' accumulated offenses against the *time* of Odysseus, most students who are initially troubled by Odysseus's vengeance come to see that the offenses against him are so great that the code of the *agathoi* binds him to refuse the gifts offered by the suitors (22.54–59; an act paralleled by Achilleus's refusal of Agamemnon's gifts) and to extract full recompense—*tinesthai*—by killing them all.

Given the central importance of *arete*, a wronged *agathos* naturally set the highest priority on obtaining recompense and restoring his *arete* even if by violence. This cultural truth provides students with the key not only to Odysseus's vengeance but also to Achilleus's wrath. For if the other Greeks cannot convince either Odysseus or Achilleus to cooperate, their claim to act as they please in restoring their honor is stronger than any other claim.

To view the Homeric poems from such a perspective allows our students to experience important and often neglected aspects of these oral epics. But how much do we lose by such an approach? Finally, I think, very little. As teachers, however, we need to be cautious. As Adam Parry realized, in studies of oral formulaic composition such historical reconsideration "can only illuminate our understanding if it derives from, and eventually adds to, a conception of Homer itself not based on a purely historical perspective, but on a recognition, in the *Iliad* and the *Odyssey*, of an artistic order and a human significance not limited to any time or place" (M. Parry, *Making* 1x). We need not let our students forget that what we see of human beings in Homer is, in essence, little different from what we see today. Patterns shift and change, but much that is fundamentally human remains. And, indeed, the tragic moral of the *Iliad* suggests that love, honor, pride, and above all the awareness of human mortality, though enmeshed in unique cultural forms, are as recognizable across the centuries as they were across the battle lines on the plains of Troy.

NOTES

[1]In my quotations from the poems, translations appear after the transliterated Greek words. The translations are by Lattimore, and I have included them along with the transliterated Greek to help the reader recall the general rendering of the Greek terms. I believe the discussion before and after each quotation makes explicit the actual Greek usage.

[2]For a better understanding of the role of tradition in the composition and transmission of the Homeric poems, see Kirk, *Homer and the Oral Tradition*, ch. 4, and Havelock, chs. 4–5.

[3]Adkins discusses his method most concisely in "Classical Studies: Has the Past a Future?" He applies the method to texts from classical Athens but reviews Homeric culture as the origin of much classical value-word usage. The Loeb Classical Library

versions of the Homeric poems (trans. A. T. Murray) offer a convenient way to identify the Greek words used in selected passages.

[4]My discussion of both the descriptive and evaluative ranges of value words, and of the competitive and cooperative virtues, is heavily indebted to Adkins's work in *Moral Values* 6–9 and in "Classical Studies." I have also consulted his *Merit and Responsibility* 1–60 and *From the Many to the One* 1–48. Adkins's work on Greek moral values has been criticized by K. J. Dover and A. A. Long. Dover objects to Adkins's argument on two counts. First, Dover argues that Adkins has unjustifiably limited the number and range of value words in his analysis. Second, Dover believes that Adkins overemphasizes the notion of a ranking of evaluative words. Many non-competitive evaluative words conflict with competitive words, Dover asserts, but are not necessarily "higher" or "lower" in ethical significance. Long, while acknowledging "considerable indebtedness" to Adkins's work, expresses "grave doubts about the appropriateness in principle of attempting to classify Homeric ethical terminology under the two exclusive categories" of competitive or cooperative values (123). Long specifically worries that Adkins has not given adequate weight to Homeric criticism of *excess* or *deficiency* in behavior. He admits that competitive and cooperative values "may clash" but counters that there are examples in Homer of significant attempts to link those values.

Homeric Epic and the Social Order

Michael N. Nagler

> This speech [Hektor's prayers for his son] comes from
> a god-doomed man whose city is under siege, whose
> patrimony is imperiled, and whose family face
> imminent enslavement by enemies animated by
> precisely the same warrior values.
>
> Alvin Gouldner

> But here [in the *Odyssey*] is no mere folktale; here are
> full-grown people, crafty, subtle, and passionate.
>
> Virginia Woolf

What is the *Odyssey* about? The question can be answered in at least three ways, all of them valid:

1. It is a story of *identity*. Even the ancient critics recognized this, for as Dio Chrysostom flatly states, "pasa he epopeia anagnorisis" 'the entire epic is a recognition scene' (cf. Aristotle, *Poetics* 24.14596 15). Since antiquity many readers have been aware that Homer's preoccupation with the revelation, falsification, investigation, recognition, and (as in the "No-man" trick in the Cyclops's cave) mockery of identity is much more than a dramatic device or formal requirement of the ubiquitous guest-friendship conventions (*xenia*); it is a deep philosophical sounding of the first problem of human existence, who we are.

Naturally, Homer treats the question from the perspective of the archaic period and uses the thematic resources of traditional oral narrative. For example, Odysseus's *anagnorisis* with Penelope: at this climax of a major plot component of the poem, the hero furnishes his wife with final proof of his identity by recounting at some length how he built their marriage bed out of—or, rather, onto—a still-living olive tree. Clearly he is identifying who he is, not only individually but typologically, not only as a man who shares a secret with her and one other human being but as a man capable of building order out of nature (without, we might add, killing nature in the process), grounding in the renewable life of the earth, family life and the economic and political life that depends on family structure. Students who see the stress that Homer places at this moment on the typological side of the hero's identity are often on their way to appreciating the balance of the generic with the particular that they must grasp before they can understand Homer, or any archaic literature in the oral style. (For this purpose,

57

it is helpful to introduce students to Mircea Eliade's concept of "archaic ontology" or, for more specialized students, to J. A. Notopoulos.)

In between the generic and the particular, the archetypal story and its vividly human and individual medium, is the rich matrix of traditional themes. In this matrix lie many explanations for many Homeric peculiarities—why, for example, the poet cannot simply have Odysseus show Penelope the proof-positive identity token—namely, the scar from an old boar wound—that works so well with Eumaios and Philoitios, with Telemachos, and later with Laertes. The hero got the wound as a young man while hunting during a formal visit to his maternal relatives on Parnassus (19.393–466). Such a scar is usually a token of initiation (see Rubin and Sale), but for a Greek male, initiation meant transference from the family context into the context of warriors and the larger community. That is the right identity to display to Eumaios, Philoitios, and Telemachos, because Odysseus is about to enlist them as allies in the battle against the suitors. But this "Iliadic" world of male camaraderie and warriorhood must be carefully circumscribed in the concluding portion of the *Odyssey*, where the agenda is precisely the hero's reintegration, as far as that is possible, with the family. Family and warrior band (*Männerbund*) are competing institutions the working out of whose tensions is a major part of Homer's program for both the epics. A display of the scar, with its associations of the male sodality, would offend Penelope and frustrate the thematic design of the *Odyssey*'s conclusion. (Note that the hero's father gets to see both the warrior and the family identities, represented by the scar and the orchard [24.331–44]).

2. The *Odyssey* is about *experience*. Forms of the word *peir-* 'test, try, experience' occur forty-two times in the poem (with two doubtful cases and five puns, by my count). All the episodes of Odysseus's wanderings, the "exotica," make sense in their extreme typological similarity, their folkloric and other forms of typological patterning (Niles, "Patterning"), and their special differences. One function of the Sirens episode, for example, is to locate the raiding hero's first serious break with warriorhood, since the Sirens tempt him with *klea andron* 'heroic song' (see *Il.* 9.189) and he does not get "sucked in." (Note his hapless attempt later to revert to a use of war gear against Skylla and Charybdis [*Od.* 12.226–233].) But another function of the episode, more generic but still relevant to this stage of Odysseus's development, is to display the three basic ways a human being can respond to the experience of strong temptation. Bleaching on the strand of the Sirens' isle are the bones of men who literally and figuratively went overboard and perished. At the other extreme, Odysseus's crew go by with their ears stuffed, blocking the experience out and in effect not having it. Only one man, the hero, has the experience fully without giving way to it. Steady at the mast of his life, he assumedly—Homer's vocabulary for psychological development is never explicit—learns and grows.

3. The *Odyssey* is about *community*. The great contemporary interest in the question of order and disorder, "rest and violence," helps us seize students' attention when we present the poems from this point of view (see Machinist; also Niles [*Beowulf*], who considers that *Beowulf*, too, is about community). Moreover, considerable new research is available that can give interesting interpretative guidelines on this issue.

The problem, as usually stated, has two sides, order and disorder (I argue that the *Odyssey* specializes in the former and the *Iliad* in the latter). Thanks to the work of scholars on early Greek society and the ancient economy, of whom Moses Finley and Alvin Gouldner are perhaps the most accessible to students, we now know, for example, why *xenia* is the controlling motif of the *Odyssey*: because the guest-host relationship contracted between social equals and embodied in reciprocal gift exchanges was the most important social relation beyond the extended family in Homer's world, the pre-state world of freely interacting but independent households (*oikoi*). Not to enter into *xenia* contracts is to impede the process of social integration—in a word, to be on the side of chaos. In the exotica, Odysseus visits "alternative societies"—or, as we would say today, different "world-order models"—testing their inhabitants (and himself) for the ability to form guest-friend contracts; then he returns home and restores the capacity of his own society to honor such contracts (see, e.g., 24.315–17, where Laertes breaks down partly because he experiences a fresh memory of Odysseus, partly because he thinks the man before him is a *xenos* whom he cannot gratify).

This simple plot outline goes far to explain the process and tension of the epic, and once the importance of the issues is understood in Homer's terms, much that seemed hardly worth the fuss—for example, the Phaiakian guest gifts Odysseus is so concerned about bringing home—becomes not only understandable but exciting.

Some scholars of the poem have noticed, I think correctly, a premonition of "polis ideology" to which Homer is reacting negatively; for example, Phaiakian civilization has been seen as "hyper-*oikos*" in its incipient civic institutions and public works, while the Cyclopes are obviously "sub *oikos*" (the political equivalent of Lévi-Strauss's "raw") in their inability to form even family clusters—not to mention *xenia* networks (9.266–80).

But if the world of external alliances is to remain loose and decentralized in Homer's view (and a reading of Benveniste 95 would explain why), nothing is more centralized than the *oikos* itself. All goods and services proceed from the *agros* (surrounding farm and grazing lands) or from the household workers to the center, that is, to the paterfamilias and his wife, for redistribution. Hence the importance of Odysseus's effect on the Phaiakian house and on his own: the moment he reveals his identity to the Phaiakians, and even sooner in Ithaka (11.336–52, 18.274–301), goods are called in for redistribution to the *xenos* by the head family (by, in fact, the wives). By his mere presence, as it were, Odysseus stimulates the economy of the *oikos* and makes the system work.

The disorder or violence side of the coin presents more difficult problems and perhaps brings us face-to-face with the poem's true ethical ambiguities. I alluded to violence against nature in the episode of the bed trick, a concern that is obviously prominent in the attack on the cattle of the sun (*Od.* 12) and the attack on the "natural," or "hypocultural," Polyphemos (*Od.* 9), each of which is labeled, consistently with the multilayered logic of oral narrative, as *the* adventure that defines Odysseus's identity and his problem (see, respectively, 1.8–9 and 11.104–17; 11.102–03). But Odysseus—"he who hurts," in the full ambiguity of that term (Dimock), the hero who "loses" his crew (the word also means "destroys") and who destroys half his society to save it—leaves us with an unsatisfied sense of the role of violence in the social or the world order. In a single example I have found instructive, the poet, summing up the condition of the suitors slaughtered by Odysseus in his hall, uses a simile that likens them to "netted fish, yielding up their life to the sun" (22.388). External evidence (see esp. the *Hymn to Apollo* 371–74 and *Il.* 21.331–41) shows this to be an image of purification: the hero who uses violence to restore the order of the household purifies society. We can be reasonably sure that this is the interpretation that the simile and other narrative elements place on Odysseus's actions. But is it true? (Here reference to Girard is very helpful.) Did the poet believe it? We are left with these larger questions.

The *Iliad* is in some ways a less complicated poem than the *Odyssey*; for many students today it is less interesting, and it certainly can be less appealing. Yet it deals with the same themes and is governed by the same concern. If the *Odyssey* describes the restoration of the social order and the underlying cosmic order, the *Iliad* shows us how the social order is destroyed (while the cosmic order is threatened, but prevails). Students should not miss the significance of the anxiety voiced by Aidoneus, the death god, when Achilleus's rampage is placing the social and divine universe under maximum stress: Aidoneus fears that his realm will "break open to the sight of men and gods in its choking dankness" (20.64–65). A special meaning of this threat is shaped in Indo-European ideology, since the "hordes of the dead" were the mythological symbolic code for the rampaging warrior sodality (*Männerbund*) that did, in fact, at times engulf the social order in the form of a vigilante mob or praetorian corps gone out of control. (Many students will be familiar with this mythology through the ride of the Rohan in Tolkien's imaginative Ring trilogy; but for a more historical discussion, see Benveniste 1: 302–03).

The life styles of Achilleus and Odysseus perfectly reflect the social commitments of the two epics. Odysseus is a family man, at least of the archaic, patriarchal variety, while Achilleus feels himself to be driven by priorities that sweep away from him the possibility of settled life (18.79–83). For the poems are based on two antithetical values, compassion (*eleos*) and glory (*kleos*), that Homer, and archaic society, never succeeded in reconciling. Compassion can be fully realized only in a society that is balanced and whole with respect to the complementary functions of men and women, while glory—given its competitive definition among the Greeks—gravitates to an arena of unrestricted competition among exclusively male individuals, that is, war. These two worlds and their values collide briefly at the Skaian gates in book 6 of the *Iliad*, only to show us the rejection of *eleos* that the impact of the Achaian raiding expedition imposes even on the defending Trojans (Arthur). But the dimensions of the *Iliad* tragedy go deeper and wider than this effect. By the time Achilleus feels sufficiently vindicated to respond to *eleos* and release Hektor's body, it will be too late not only for Hektor and Patroklos but for Achilleus himself, whose imminent death is caused by choices and events within the poem. It will be too late as well for Troy and the apparent victors, perhaps the entire civilization they represent, since the Achaian centers of "Argos, Sparta, and broad-wayed Mykenai," in what may be Homer's attempt to account for the historical disaster of the Bronze Age states, are also programmed for destruction, by the dreadful compact between Zeus and Hera in book 4 (5–56). There will be no winners in the Trojan War.

What human flaw lies at the heart of all this tragic loss? For myself, as for several other contemporary scholars, it is the competitive definition of excellence, which was so characteristically—but far from exclusively—Greek. For Achilleus, the contradiction comes to a head in the embassy episode of book 9 where he seems unable to gratify his "friends" without also signaling his submission to his loathsome "enemy" of the moment, Agamemnon. He thus finds himself in a trap that engineers him into certain death and that, I have argued, upsets Homer to the extent that he has difficulties managing the narrative structure of the scene.

The foregoing is my overview of the epics as it has evolved so far. In teaching, one attempts not to impose but simply expose such an overview to students in order to stimulate without unduly predetermining their responses to these great literary monuments. For that purpose the approach I have illustrated above has worked well, mutatis mutandis, at undergraduate and graduate levels.

In conclusion, the Homeric epos was built up in three levels of semantic organization, if we may so generalize. Every reader first encounters a web of well-differentiated human individuals—"full-grown people, crafty, subtle, and passionate"—acting out a vivid and well-articulated story. Later one begins to perceive that a rich inherited substratum of theme and ideology is also working itself out as a "subtext" of themes not specific to individuals or given narrative moments but part of inherited Indo-European and other ideologies responding to the strategies of orally performed epic narration (Nagy; Nagler). In this substratum most of the apparent inconsistencies of the performance are explained away or at least accounted for, the text yields most readily to interpretation, and scholarly methods are most required for analysis. Finally, as with any serious literary work, a level of universal signification is unmistakable. Odysseus is a real person, all right; he is also the creator of balance between culture and nature; the defender of *xenia*, suppliancy, and the other socially ordering strategies; a traditionalist who defends central authority where archaic opinion wanted it defended while he resists its subordination to a political order more impersonal, formalized, and inevitable; a defeater of chaos. And he is Everyman Triumphant—the Walter Mitty within each of us, perpetually making it.

The Homeric epics are unusual in their combination of complexity and coherence. Whether the result of the stability of the tradition, the brilliance of our performer, or, as I believe, of both, it is this combination that makes him most rewarding to explore and teach.

Homeric Icons

Norman Austin

It is a universal human experience that the world presents itself to us in two different modes that are opposed yet, in mysterious ways, related to each other. All cultures, whether primitive or sophisticated, recognize these two modes, though the vocabulary for expressing them will vary greatly from culture to culture. The one mode presents the world as a system of facts. This is the world of ordinary, daily life. It is the world of sense perceptions and of deductive reasoning, of regularity and predictability. In this world cause and effect are as surely related as the sequence of the seasons. In this mode the laws of natural phenomena prevail, and also the laws that govern social relations. In this mode the world is knowable. In the second mode the world resists knowing and yet demands to be known. The uncanny, the weird, the unpredictable, the random, chance, fate, destiny, are terms that this mode generates. In this mode the world presents itself as opaque and mysterious. Though it too asserts cause and effect, the connection between them is elusive, as if there were a gap, a disjunction, between them. Much as certain subatomic particles apparently vanish into nothingness and come back into being somewhere else, in this mode cause vanishes and mysteriously reappears as effect in an unexpected location. In this mode the world presents itself not as a system of facts but as a system of signs. It speaks through intimations, intuitions, dreams, epiphanies, and revelations.

We might call these two modes the physical and the metaphysical, except that even modern physics cannot avoid reproducing the two modes in its cosmology. The table is a physical event, visible, durable, and solid. Yet what could be more meta-physical than the atoms and their charmed particles, whose motions beyond the threshold of our senses cause the table to have its visible form and palpable mass? We could as well call the two modes the practical and the theoretical. For practical purposes it will do to call a line a series of points, but theory knows no mathematics of infinitesimals that can link one point with another to generate a continuum. Between one point and the next is an abyss as vast as our galaxy. One mode presents the world in parts; it is incremental, digital, even though the world it constructs seems stable and continuous. The second mode is holistic, though its appearances are fragmentary, partial, and provisional. Events in the one mode can be diagrammed; events in the other mode can only be represented by icons.

In all cultures the dialectic between the two modes is complex since each declares itself the mode of the real, yet neither can exist without the other.

In Homer's cosmology the two modes are structured as the world of the gods and the world of human affairs—all social relations, thought, action, attitudes, aspirations, and emotions. From our historical perspective we can see that what Homer presents with all the vividness and truth of physical reality are projections onto the cosmos of these two modes of psychic perception. The two modes, in modern psychological theory, are the conscious and the unconscious. Homer's gods, standing at the threshold between the two planes, partake of both. They are icons, representations of that world beyond the senses, beyond the reason and conscious thought that sense perception builds from its data base. They are also the guardians of the threshold, placed there to hold the territory of the suprasensuous inviolate from the rash incursions of the conscious ego. They act as the controls on human aspirations and conduct. At the same time they are the signifiers pointing human consciousness to the system beyond consciousness that, though hidden, elusive, and seemingly capricious, determines the forms of physical reality as they appear to conscious thought. The gods occupy the liminal zone between the conscious and the unconscious, as presences that span the gap and close the circuit.

In Homer the workings of the gods are not apparent to normal human sight, in other words, to the conscious mind. One hero or another may receive a momentary epiphany, when a god assumes a form acceptable to the hero's consciousness. But not even the greatest of the heroes can tell us of the councils of the gods, of their deliberations, their disputes, their competitions or concordats. Only a seer has privileged access to this realm, and Homer is our seer. Homer's vision can transport us to the realm of cosmic events beyond conscious perception and reason. Are the humans autonomous in their actions or are they at the mercy of the gods' whims? The question is useful, indeed inevitable, yet inadequate if left in that form. It suggests that gods and humans inhabit separate worlds, when in fact they inhabit the same world and everything they do has reference to only one world, the world of here and now. The question itself comes from the conscious mind, prompted by digital thinking. It cannot be answered in that form, since it is addressed precisely to that point where digital thought exhausts itself and founders in the numinous. The modern model of the dialectic of conscious and unconscious gives us an instrument for observing human motivation and responsibility in Homer's cosmology. Both models, the Homeric and the modern psychological, are hypothetical, of course, and as theoretical systems they will not overlap point for point. The advantage of applying the psychoanalytic model to Homer, however, is that the modern model takes as its premise that gods and humans inhabit not separate worlds but one world, which is the human mind, and that the two sets of terms are projections of two modes of knowing, each of which is incomplete without the other. Readers of Homer may prefer models other than the psychoanalytic for understanding the complementarity of the divine and the human. Whatever the model, it must be able to encompass the actions of the humans and the gods in a single force field. Homer's cosmology presents a unified field theory. As modern interpreters we must measure Homer's accomplishment with a model adequate to that unity.

The Homeric landscape is dominated by the gods. The gods in subsequent European poetry may strike us as some kind of metaphorical presence, but in Homer their presence is so dynamic, palpable, physical, so integrated into human affairs, that we cannot bring ourselves to call them mere machinery. Plato was disturbed at Homer's portrait of human behavior but even more disturbed by the unexemplary behavior of his deities, opulent in their desires, moods, and acts. Far from joining with Plato to banish Homer from our cities, we require our young to study the Homeric poems as if they were sources of wisdom and guides to life. On the other hand, we do not really believe in these archaic gods, at least not as Homer and his audience must have believed in them. History has, as it were, removed Plato's chief objection to the Homeric cosmology, yet what is Homer without his gods? Why read Homer at all if we can so easily dismiss the persons who are not casual stage machinery but the very agents of destiny throughout the poems? If Homer has the moral authority to warrant our placing him on the required-reading lists, we must know where we stand in relation to those imperious, jealous, vindictive, graceful, quarrelsome, devious powers and forces that motivate and thwart all the human actions in his poems.

One approach, the humanistic approach, is to note the correspondences between human and divine motivation. Achilleus is innately heroic, we say, and the gods reinforce the traits already present in his genes. Odysseus is innately resourceful, versatile, and cunning, and Athene reinforces just these traits. Paris is innately effeminate and cowardly, and Aphrodite, in pulling him from the battlefield back to the bedroom, only accomplishes an action to which his own intentions would naturally gravitate. This way of seeing Homeric motivation is correct. The gods do not make Achilleus a coward; they do not make Odysseus forget his cunning or Paris his esthete's vanity. Yet if we stop here we are not so much entering into Homeric theology as excusing it, finding Homer *almost* a humanist, with a perception that could *almost* have dispensed with the divine machinery. A moment's thought reveals the inadequacy of this position. Yes, we could excise the gods from the text, and Achilleus would still rage, Odysseus still pry into caves and grottoes, Paris still vanish from the battlefield, Agamemnon still drift like a somnambulist through his responsibilities, Hektor still defend his brother to the death. Everything would be the same, and it would all be completely different. Who would want the Homeric landscape to be thus expurgated?

Those great Olympian presences that haunt the Homeric poems have enchanted readers and listeners of all ages ever since the poems were first sung. Plato well understood that Homer's powers of enchantment found their most powerful expression in those icons feeding on ambrosia on the Olympian heights. Bulldoze Olympos off the map and who of us, however modern, however mature, would care to give Homer a second glance? We might as well start from a position of honesty. We love the Homeric gods. We do not want to rid the poems of their beguiling presence. We want them. We love them for their interventions, their cross-purposes, their contradictions, their misty epiphanies, their carefree immortality, their radiance, their thunder. Every reader of Homer falls in love with Homer's gods. What we want, if we are not to banish Homer, together with his morally dubious authorities, from our civilized community, is to continue to enjoy our love affair with his gods in a way that will not too grossly offend our modern scientific and humanistic scruples.

Freud and all his successors in psychoanalysis and psychology, whatever their affiliation, have shown us just such an avenue, whereby we can love those archaic gods, give them their due, and still retain the critical stance of a mature judgment. Psychoanalysis has given back to us our soul that was in danger of disappearing under the advancing tide of scientific rationalism. We have, albeit reluctantly, learned to withdraw personifications from the outer cosmos and to diagram it with vectors of abstract forces—gravity, electromagnetism, chemical bonding, genetic coding. But the soul has not disappeared, however much we may mouth the language of the behavioral sciences. We are still individual and collective bundles of feelings, hopes, fears, intentions, desires, imaginings, motivations, choices, which the behavioral sciences cannot yet reduce entirely to chemical interactions. Freud and his successors began to uncover the workings of this seat of passions and yearnings that we now commonly call the psyche. Not all the workings are equally lovely, but one reason for the soul's fall from favor in modern times was the Christian insistence on the soul as only beautiful. The Christians were Platonists. Psychoanalysis discovered that the true therapy of the soul was to bring forward for conscious acknowledgment the obscure inner, and even the sordid lower, workings that Plato and Platonic Christians had thought to exclude from the perfected, ideal Soul.

The Homeric pantheon is the soul, or at least its outer structure. We can see the connection more clearly now that we have withdrawn personification from the elements and the natural forces of wind, water, sun, and light. The Homeric pantheon is the skeleton, the nervous system, and the delicate membrane enclosing us within the soul, or the soul within us, according to our orientation to this most substantial and immaterial essence. Once we see the Homeric pantheon in this light, we can accept such gods, we can find our love for them acceptable, even when we do not find them always exemplary, because in them we can read written large the dynamic motions of our own souls.

In Freud's psychic cosmology the superego holds a near impregnable position on the heights, from which it surveys the actions of the ego below, always poised to scold, punish, deflect, praise, or reward. What are Homer's Olympians but that imperious superego? As superpowers they are absolute. They are the values of the Homeric society, housed behind the clouds in the folds of Olympos, invisible yet always present, always reprimanding or prompting, guardians of the collective morality, demanding from the mortals below obedience to a moral code that they themselves seem able to flout with impunity. Alain, speaking of these superpowers, has put into the mouth of Socrates an instructive fiction. Once upon a time, says the shade of Socrates to Alain, humans lived among giants whose wants were supplied without labor, who lived in such abundance that they freely gave of their goods to whoever knew how to please them.

> So it came about, [says the shade of Socrates,] that men never thought of working, nor of walking, nor of building wagons or ships; instead they became natural orators, and spent all their time watching the giants, figuring out what would please them or displease them, smiling at them or imploring them with tears in their eyes, or else simply pronouncing the necessary words, which had to be memorized exactly, though they had no understanding of the changes of humor that would come over the giants, their brusque refusals, or their sudden willing-ness.   (Alain 23–24)

Yes, the Olympian gods are the giants that we, from our cradles, where all fantasies arise, have projected onto the cosmic landscape. Homer even adds perhaps to Freud's image of the superego by revealing, through the polytheistic model, the contradictions in the superego. In the actions and moods of the Homeric gods we see a constellation of father images. We see the authoritarian patriarch; the father turbulent in his emotional reversals; the distant, the angry, the secretive, the admiring, the demanding father. The mother images are as numerous and varied. Homer gives us the shrew; the devious wife; the radiantly beautiful mother; the conspiring, the inspir-ing, the gracious, the protective, the emancipated (relatively), the submis-sive, the punitive mother. And in the crosscurrents that sweep through the councils on Olympos we read the contradictions in the authority figures we, too, project onto those remote heights. Yes, these are the gods we project from our cradles as we watch the giants passing to and fro. Their antics, gestures, poses, their inexplicable appearances and disappearances, their tempers, their clouded intentions, their awesome stature, their handsome capable physiques, their wealth, their generosity, their bewildering ambiguity, their autonomy, their serenity, knowledge, power, immortality, all these Homer recorded with amazing fidelity to our childhood projections from the cradle.

Did Freud talk of the complications of the superego? If not, Homer's portrait makes good the omission. In Homer's superpowers we see the ego's projection of what it would like to be but cannot. His superpowers inhabit a world from which death, disease, and deprivation are absent. Incest is permitted them; adultery, even rape, are acceptable. Action at a distance, unlimited resources, mobility, magical powers, all these traits of Homer's superpowers are the ego's desires personified in the form of gods whose liberties the ego aspires to but cannot attain. The first level of the superego is simply a grander version of the ego, the infant ego's vision of the powers it might and should have, were it not thwarted by its own frailty and dependence.

Well, if the ego is too frail to attain its desires, it must build for itself a fortress and conscript warriors to hold the fortress against attackers. Into the superego it constructs another level, an Olympian military post to which it can repair in times of danger. A priest, vexed by the insults of a warrior, can invoke by magic formulas an avenging demon, and Apollo, swollen with the anger transferred from priest to god, strides down the mountainside to devastate the Greek army with the plague. A warrior, insulted in his manhood by the alpha male, repairs to the solitary beach, and his tears of humiliation invoke his mother, a sea goddess of surpassing beauty, with the power to persuade heaven's supreme ruler to ally himself with her ego-bound son and spread confusion in the mind of the enemy. We call them gods, the Olympian inhabitants, but they are demons, too, that the ego, by scrupulous magical formulas, can conjure up to carry out its devious injunctions, retaliatory missions against other egos intervening between it and its desires.

Then there is the superego who turns suddenly in retaliation on the ego itself when the ego steps incautiously beyond its bounds. A puny fellow bent on raising hell adventures into a cave brimming with milk and cheese. Against his comrades' protests, he lingers until the occupant returns, an ugly ogre with a single penetrating eye and an enormous club. The little fellow manages by wit and advanced technology to escape from the giant's grasp but, ego-bound to the end, cannot refrain from identifying himself; he thereby incurs the anger of Poseidon, which buffets him around the Mediterranean for ten years and haunts him for the rest of his life (Austin, "Odysseus"). A silly commander places his own prerogatives above his responsibilities to his warriors, and Zeus befuddles his brain with a foolish dream, an example of wish fulfillment if ever there was one; the dream says that, in spite of the commander's irresponsible actions, the rising mutiny in his army, and the plague's devastation, the fool can expect to walk out and take the walled city of Troy the very next day. Foolish adventurers stray into an enchanted copse, and the enchantress transforms hearty fellows into swinish brutes. In these instances the superego appears in its punitive forms to check an ego overly avaricious.

The superego is so often simply an ego enlarged, the ego's wish fulfillment fantasized as figures of greater power, greater privilege, figures who are larger, freer, more wilful, more capricious than the ego can or dares to be, that we must not forget that beyond its ego pretensions, its complicity with the ego, it is also the conscience. Zeus, for all his promiscuity, is still the guardian of justice, whose will and mind coincide with destiny itself. Athene, for all her duplicity, is foresight and wisdom. Aphrodite, for all her scheming, is love and beauty. Apollo, as Chryses's demon, is gorged with his priest's anger, yet he is also the manifestation of justice, natural law operating to bring about a disease in an army that has recklessly abused the land on which it is encamped and that has ignored the practices of basic sanitation. Homer's gods are all too human, human in all the human ways of failing, but they are also the ideal, agents of the natural order, expressions of natural laws, mysterious, often terrifying, gracious too, but always inexorable. Somewhat dimly, awkwardly, tentatively they seem to be groping toward that space beyond the ego where an impersonal but natural justice prevails. In their palaces on Olympos they indulge themselves in a luxury that the ego can attain only in dreams. But beyond their indulgence they shine forth as ideals, ideals in the making, though still clotted with earthly motives; ideals of courage, honesty, civility, beauty, intelligence, and love; the dream of an ego satisfied in its private wants and reaching for a vocabulary adequate to the transpersonal, transcendent state.

If the Olympian superpowers are what modern psychology can group together as the superego, the Homeric hero is the ego itself. As polymorphous as its greater and better half, the ego parades through Homer's rank-and-file hexameters as now a dandy, now a veteran given to garrulous anecdotes of past campaigns, now a cuckold, now an incompetent commander, now a wily strategist, now a conscientious objector from the ranks pummeled back into submission, now as a war brave, glorious in his plumes, loyal, constant in battle, and infantile in his appetite for the ribbons of honor. Apart from the specification that we must simply accept, that in Homer's warrior society heroes are male by definition and woman is, if we like, the anima to support the manly ego, Homer's roster of warriors yields a whole schoolhouse of ego types, rambunctious youngsters competing with and against each other for their share of the world's goods—sexual prizes, livestock, precious metals, and the more precious illusion of honor.

If the gods represent the value system (Diel), heroes are the society's representatives to whom is given the quest to define those values, to assimilate and embody them. Courage in battle, stamina in a sea storm, clever thinking in an ogre's cave, prudent deliberations in councils, suave repartee at court, all are instances of the ego's attempt to reconstruct itself into the image of the gods that it has created to be the image of itself. The image of the gods is the first and greatest act of human consciousness (Soleri), for by imaging the gods we become conscious of ourselves, conscious then of our task, which is to become one with our gods. The *Iliad* is the tragic vision of this consciousness, the poet's keening lament for an ego that, endowed with the noblest mettle (without the nobility, no tragedy: Aristotle), aspiring to the loftiest sublimation, falters and careers into an orgy of destruction. Unable to assimilate the values correctly, unable to sublimate, to reach the sublime heights where it has posted its supreme values, the ego surrenders to the infernal forces of anger and hate, and everywhere the gold it reaches for turns to dust. In the *Odyssey* the ego, against all odds, against all expectations, in spite of serious flaws in judgment, stupid moves, ignorance, laziness, acts of aggression against innocent victims, finds its way home, becomes nested again in the embrace of the images it had projected out into the wide world to light its way back to its self.

Shall we call Homer a primitive for populating his world with such infantile images—Olympian idols often as ego-bound as their makers and human warriors given over to lust, aggression, plunder, having the appetites of a child and fantasizing great gods to approve and enlarge such appetites? Only if we can claim we have evolved beyond the infant state ourselves. The evidence suggests we have not. Newspapers, television, magazines, movies, the media show us a world no different from Homer's. Call our gods what you will, when the issue is between honor and aliveness, we will choose to stand on our honor, even if it is an empty honor celebrated on the rubble field of a planet destroyed by our insatiable vanity. In a world where unconsciousness is by great acclamation preferred to consciousness, Homer's vision of the human spirit growing up into the consciousness of itself is a beacon we do well to cherish.

The Concept of the Hero

John E. Rexine

The *Iliad* and the *Odyssey* of Homer stand as the earliest literary monuments of the Western world and as the most representative and most nearly perfect examples in European literature of the orally composed epic. They belong to a literary genre that has been largely replaced today by the novel, despite the efforts of Nikos Kazantzakis, in his monumental *Odyssey* of 33,333 lines, to resuscitate that literary form for contemporary readers. For all practical purposes, Homer created the epic (the Greek word *epos* means "the uttered word"), though he stands at a point in the history of the oral Greek tradition that saw a long process come to fruition (Vivante *Epithets*). In modern terms, the Homeric epic was a long national, narrative poem in dactylic hexameters, handed down from generation to generation, that became for the ancient Greeks what the Bible was for the ancient Hebrews (Rexine, *Hellenic Spirit* 1–7).

As epic poems both the *Iliad* and the *Odyssey* have central heroes (Frame 116–24), and it is important in teaching the poems to examine the concept of hero (Nagy). The main heroes help account for the enduring appeal of these epics and their story lines. Even though women were never to achieve as high a social status in any period in Greek history as they did in Homeric times, it is substantially a male-oriented, male-dominated, patriarchal world that we shall be examining. But the success of such cinematic delights as *Superman* I, II, and III would seem to suggest that the macho male hero has yet to lose his appeal in twentieth-century America, and members of both sexes look to heroes or (now) heroines in one way or another, even if only in their imaginations. Heroic poetry is not accidentally so called, though each of us may have a different view of what constitutes a hero. The Greek word *heros*, from which our English word is derived, can be found in Homer himself. Among the definitions of hero that come to mind are the five categories found in the second edition of *Webster's New Twentieth Century Unabridged Dictionary*:

> 1. in mythology and legend, a man of great strength and courage, favored by the gods and in part descended from them, often regarded as a half-god and worshiped after his death; as Aeneas and Hector were *heroes* to the ancients; 2. any man admired for his courage, nobility, or exploits, especially in war; as Washington is a national hero; 3. any person admired for his qualities or achievements and regarded as an ideal or model; 4. the central male character in a novel, play, poem,

etc., with whom the reader or audience is supposed to sympathize; protagonist: often opposed to villain. 5. the central figure in any important event or period, honored for outstanding qualities.

The student of Homer will undoubtedly come to the Homeric texts with some of these definitions vaguely in mind, but some fundamental observations should be made about the Homeric texts and their attitude toward life.

It has often been said that the Greeks created the gods in their own image and that the Hebrews posited a God who created humankind in his own image. It is important for students to realize that even though divinities play a role in the Homeric world, the Greek world is anthropocentric; the Hebrew world theocentric. Two passages—chapter 40 in the Book of Isaiah and book 6, lines 144–50, in the *Iliad*—encapsulate these two views. The passage in *Iliad*, often called the key to the poem, contains the answer Glaukos gives to the very Greek question of who he is:

> As is the generation of leaves, so is that of humanity,
> The wind scatters the leaves on the ground, but the live timber
> burgeons with leaves again in the season of spring returning.
> So one generation of men will grow while another dies.
>
> (146–50; trans. Lattimore)

In this simile spring can be taken to symbolize the resurgence of humanity, our basic indestructibility, our immortality as a species. By linking human growth with the appearance of spring, or, rather, by linking it to what seems to be an eternal constant, Homer suggests that as long as spring exists, humankind will also exist. The symbolism in line 147 indicates that the author believed that the forces with which we are always in conflict, particularly those created by nature, may succeed in scattering a few leaves from the tree but that the live timber, our minds and souls, will remain forever to regenerate new leaves and branches, or, again interpreting symbolically, new civilizations will arise as well as new, fresh societies from the old. As Plato would have agreed, human beings are mortal but humanity is immortal. Homer's primary concern, then, is with the world of humanity and its uniqueness (Rexine, "Homer").

In book 11 of the *Odyssey*, often referred to as "the book of the dead" (*nekyia*), Odysseus visits the underworld and comes on the ghost of the great hero Achilleus—certainly the most distinguished and most powerful of the Greek warriors—and says:

> Achilleus,
> no man before has been more blessed than you, nor ever
> will be. Before, when you were alive, we Argives honored you

as we did the gods, and now in this place you have great authority over the dead. Do not grieve, even in death, Achilleus. (482–86)

He gets in reply:

> O shining Odysseus, never try to console me for dying. I would rather follow the plow as thrall to another man, one with no land allotted him and not much to live on, than be a king over all the perished dead. (488–91)

In contrast to theocentric or otherworldly Near Eastern cultures (Gordon), the Greek view, the Homeric view, places the human being at the center. It is what is done in this life that is important. The Homeric concept of the hero emphasizes individuality, individual performance and choice, in marked contrast to, say, the Roman view, in which the hero is subordinated to the state and enjoined by the gods to carry out a mission that is much more important (cf. Aeneas) than any individual choice or achievement (Eliot 68). The ultimate goal of such a hero is set by others. The Homeric view stresses individual achievement, and later Greek culture continues this emphasis. At the heart of this emphasis, which forms the basis of Western humanism, is *arete* (Jaeger 3–14).

Arete is the most characteristic attribute of the Homeric hero. It can be translated as "merit," "excellence," even "self-fulfillment." In book 6.208 of the *Iliad* appears the injunction "aien aristeuein kai hypeirochon emmenai allon" 'always to be the best and to be superior to others'—an admittedly elitist goal, the sign of an aristocracy. Homer's heroes are *aristoi* ("members of the aristocracy," "aristocrats," "the best"), and they perform deeds called *aristeia*, which in the *Iliad* are outstanding military exploits. In *Humanism: The Greek Ideal and Its Survival* Moses Hadas appropriately observes:

> The most striking single feature of the Homeric ethos is the enormous importance attached to individual prowess, individual pride, individual reputation. Heroes of other epics prize their individuality also, but in none is the drive for self-assertion so ruthless and pride so paramount as in Homer. In Roman or Christian or Indian epic it is a function of heroism to submit individuality, however grandiose, to a higher sanction; the Homeric hero may not compromise loyalty to his own being with loyalty to any other, human or divine. (15)

The obvious Homeric heroic model is Achilleus, and the stature of all other Homeric heroes can be measured by Achilleus's greatness. What characterizes an *aristos* is *arete*, and what motivates the Homeric hero is a desire for the *kleos* ("glory") and the *time* ("honor") that were granted to him by his peers in recognition of his *arete*. The Homeric sense of duty is called *aidos*, and anyone can appeal to it. A violation of *aidos* arouses *nemesis*, the public sense of, or indignation at, a wrong done by the hero (Rexine, "Nature" 1–6). As Werner Jaeger aptly puts it, for the Homeric hero, "The denial of honor due one's *arete* was the greatest of human tragedies" (9).

Cedric H. Whitman in his remarkable book *Homer and the Heroic Tradition* calls Achilleus the "zenith of the heroic assumption" (162). Whitman sees that "the highest heroes are not men of delusion. They are men of clarity and purity, who will a good impossible in the world and eventually achieve it, through suffering, in their own spiritual terms" (199). At the same time, "personal integrity in Achilles achieves the form and authority of immanent divinity, with its inviolable, lonely singleness, half repellent because of its almost inhuman austerity, but irresistible in its passion and perfected selfhood" (182). Recently W. Thomas MacCary seemed to suggest that Achilleus represents a primitive stage in human development that involves a childlike narcissistic reversion that is aware of maternal anaclisis. This reading of Homer may seem preposterous to some, but it implies that the story of the Homeric hero embodies "the principle that ontogeny recapitulates phylogeny" (259). MacCary has reformulated a Hegelian critical system in which "our self-appreciation of Achilleus's experience of seeking self-consciousness resolves that moment and the moment of our own infantile experience into the notion of self-consciousness itself" (239). This kind of interpretation posits a Homeric hero who is wild, rapacious, aggressive, and so self-centered that he gives rise to the appellation "Achilles complex." More simplistic, perhaps, but more useful is Kenneth Atchity's claim that "the theme in the *Iliad* is the relationship between order and disorder on all levels, from the most personal to the most widely social, from the human to the divine" (xv). Achilleus becomes the hero who preserves and restores order: "Out of chaotic divine forces Zeus personally creates order by his Olympian law; Hephaistos creates an image of that order; Achilles (with increasing insight) sees and imitates the order of the shield; and we are to imitate Achilles" (xiv). The Homeric hero is thus seen as restoring proper order by destroying those forces that disrupt it.

It is, of course, in book 9 of the *Iliad*—the famous "embassy" book, in which Aias, Odysseus, and Achilleus's tutor, Phoinix, come to Achilleus to urge him to return to battle—that Phoinix outlines the process of Homeric education (*paideia*) that every hero must undergo through *gnome* ("the general teaching," "the principle") and through the *paradeigma* (historical or mythological example), reminding us that *arete* can be defined also as the ability to use words and to perform deeds. Then follow the allegory of the prayers, the story of Meleagros, and the warning not to commit an act of hubris. From the Phoinix passage it is clear that definition of *arete*, which was equivalent originally to warlike prowess, has broadened to suit a developing aristocratic ideal. (Students should be reminded that most of the classical Greek and Roman literature that has come down to us is aristocratic.)

In the *Odyssey* it is intellectual ability that is exalted. Odysseus's *arete* is his intellectual ability, his intelligence, and he is constantly inspired by his divine companion and protector, Athene, the goddess of intelligence (Jaeger 6). Though the *Odyssey* is technically a *nostos* or "return" poem, an oral epic like the *Iliad*, it is concerned with the return of the hero to his home in Ithaka (Frame 34–80), with a human being who may mean many things to many people (Austin, *Archery*). The hero represents humankind in its supreme form, a combination of physical strength, intellectual ability, and the will to survive all obstacles, all odds. The *Odyssey* is ultimately a tribute to the survivability of humankind through the astute use of intelligence, and though modern feminists might wish to castigate it as a poem with a chauvinist hero, it has been shown that Odysseus's counterpart, Penelope, possesses just as much intelligence and survival power as Odysseus does (J. Finley, *Homer's* Odyssey 1–24). Throughout the epic Odysseus preserves his humanity, always recognizing his human limitations, his mortality, and never yielding to the temptation of hubris. Even when Kalypso offers him immortality if he will stay with her, he refuses, longing only to return home (5.214–24). Odysseus is not tempted, for he knows that only the gods and goddesses are blessed with immortality and that to aspire to be a divinity would be an act of hubris (*Od.* 1.32–43). Odysseus, it should be noted, is delayed by divine females; his dalliances are not in response to claims made on him by human females.

Both Achilleus and Odysseus are heroic figures who are driven to loneliness in their search for self-fulfillment. John Finley appropriately comments, "Achilles at the end of the *Iliad* has been forced toward loneliness; as seen at the start of the *Odyssey*, Odysseus has long reached that state. Homer is concerned with what a lone man must come to understand, and heroism to him is what brings a man to the acknowledgment" (*Homer's* Odyssey 72). Each hero aspires to a deeper, more meaningful knowledge of himself and of reality. Whitman puts it this way:

> Each implies a distinct view of what reality is: Odysseus sees reality as the situation or problem before him; Achilles sees it as something in himself, and the problem is to identify himself with it completely, through action. In both *Iliad* and *Odyssey*, Odysseus is fully the man of survival by adjustment. (175)

For those who may wonder how Odysseus came to be the central hero of his own epic, it is in order to note that though he is not considered the most valiant hero in the *Iliad*, he is among the nine most valiant (Agamemnon;

Achilleus; Nestor; Diomedes; Aias, son of Telamon; Aias, son of Oileus; Menelaos; Odysseus; Idomeneus—in order of popularity). Odysseus is important in diplomatic and military missions: in book 1 he takes Chryseis back to her father; in book 3 the delegation to bring back Helen consists of Menelaos and Odysseus; in book 9 the embassy to Achilleus consists of Aias, Phoinix, and Odysseus; in book 10 Odysseus and Diomedes form a spy mission. Most significant is Odysseus's outstanding performance in assemblies or councils: it is Odysseus in book 2 who stops the Greeks from returning home in response to Agamemnon's ill-timed challenge; again in book 14.83 it is Odysseus who urges the Greeks to stay, and in book 19 it is Odysseus who stops Achilleus from attacking. Already in the *Iliad* he has established a reputation as a brave warrior and wise counselor—as one who could and did save the day on critical occasions (e.g., in bk. 19.216–33). Odysseus possesses practical wisdom as well as intellectual ability. He knows when to use his brains and when to use his brawn. He is just as much a Homeric hero as Achilleus.

All the Homeric heroes are fully human but also possess an excellence—*arete*—that marks them as special. (Their special qualities are always credited to divinity, not to themselves, as Odysseus's intelligence is credited to Athene and Helen's beauty to Aphrodite.) They are conscious of their humanity and of their mortality. They know their limitations. They know how to use both physical and intellectual human resources to confront problems. They experience a certain heroic loneliness but at the same time know that as human beings they must function within human society. They know that suffering is an innate part of the human experience, and they do not avoid confronting what has to be confronted. They provide models of human action and character to be studied, admired, and even imitated. The Homeric heroes appeal to us because we recognize in them our own humanity and also the full possibilities of that humanity.

Homer in Art

Howard Clarke

The practice of illustrating Homer is almost as old as the poems themselves. For if we take 700 BC as an approximate date for the poems' composition, then it is scarcely a generation later, about 670, that we see Odysseus putting out the eye of a seated Polyphemos on a large amphora now at Eleusis. Illustrations of the *Iliad* appear somewhat later, and it is not always clear whether artists were representing scenes from that epic or from some other account of the Trojan War, but one of the earliest—and arguably Homeric —illustrations is on a Brussels vase, dated around 550 and showing Thetis comforting her son Achilleus on the death of Patroklos (19.303–54).

What is special about these vase paintings is that they already display two persistent features in the subsequent history of Homeric illustration. First, artists (understandably) favored those scenes that were dramatic, recognizable, and easily accommodated within the confines of a vase, a metope, or a sarcophagus; in the *Odyssey* preferred subjects have been Polyphemos, Circe, the Sirens, and recognition scenes from the latter half. Second, artists had little compunction about adapting Homer's text: it is not Thetis but Athene who comforts Achilleus in *Iliad* 19, but the painter, remembering Thetis's visit in 18, may have decided that a combination of the two scenes would be more moving. Another complicating factor in postclassical art is that artists took many "Homeric" incidents from Vergil's *Aeneid* and Ovid's *Metamorphoses*, more popular and accessible sources. But with these cautions in mind, teachers can still find a broad span of Homeric subjects in Western art—some faithfully reproduced by illustrators, others more creatively adapted by artists—and can use them as a unique tool of elucidation and interpretation. For the artist's visualizations compensate for the Homeric bias toward speech and action, and art's "other language" gives a richness and wholeness to Homer's often sparing descriptions. And, most important, painters and sculptors, with their personal styles and within the evolving contexts of art history, have provided a chronological and perceptually interpretive commentary on Homer, enabling modern readers to "see" the poems as they have been seen by readers before them.

The popularity of the two epics in classical Greece was matched by their increasing representation in art (Schefold). Although *Odyssey* painters generally preferred the adventure books, Erich Lessing's survey of Homer "in pictures" reproduces, in color, a Roman cameo of Zeus dispatching Athene and Hermes from book 1, reliefs of Odysseus slaying the suitors, and a red-figured scene of Telemachos conversing with Nestor that is noteworthy in the light of the relative scarcity of scenes from the Telemachy. Similarly, the hundred or so illustrations, many in color, in Stanford and Luce's *Quest for Ulysses* favor the first half of the poem, though the authors also include scenes of Odysseus (normally distinguishable in art by his conical felt cap) from the *Iliad* and from his non-Homeric career. Equally inclusive are the black-and-white illustrations in Margaret R. Scherer's *The Legends of Troy in Art and Literature*. Since the *Iliad*'s battle scenes are largely unsuited to vase painting, artists tended to choose those events that featured Achilleus, such as the quarrel with Agamemnon (1), the embassy (9), Thetis's securing of arms for him from Hephaistos (18), the killing and dragging of Hektor (22), and the interview with Priam (24). These have now all been collected, in black and white and with a German commentary, under Anneliese Kossatz-Deissmann's "Achilles" entry in the *Lexicon iconographicum*; the initial volumes of this magisterial work also reproduce annotated illustrations of the Iliadic activities of Agamemnon, Aias, Aeneas, Alexandros (Paris), and Andromache.

Homer provided subjects not only for vase paintings but also for sculpture, particularly friezes and sarcophagus reliefs, as well as for wall paintings and the minor and decorative arts, by Greek and, later, Etruscan and Roman artists. Of special importance in the history of art is a series of seven large-scale *Odyssey* frescoes (first cent. BC) from a Roman villa and now in the Vatican Library. These are among the first landscapes in Western painting and reveal a remarkable feeling for light, color, and space. Most often reproduced are one that shows the Laistrygones (not a familiar subject) hurling rocks down on Odysseus's ships and another that shows his ship at anchor before an ominous arch leading to the underworld. The custom of decorating villas with cycles of paintings from Homer seems also to have been popular at Pompeii, but apart from one showing Achilleus being forced to give up Briseis, most are too badly preserved to be usefully reproduced.

The last of these painted Homers in antiquity came from miniaturists working in Constantinople in the late fifth century AD, who decorated the "Ambrosian" manuscript of the *Iliad*. Many of the fifty-eight illuminations are in a sad state of preservation, but Ranuccio Bianchi Bandinelli's study of the genre preserves some in color that illustrate the less popular incidents, such as Odysseus and Diomedes dispatching the hapless Dolon (10) or Skamandros and his river (21). A recent history of the illuminated book also reproduces the scene from book 5 of Aphrodite complaining to Zeus that she has been wounded by Diomedes (Bland 24). The miniaturists who decorated this "Milan *Iliad*" were not particularly adept at rendering the human anatomy, so it is sometimes difficult to recognize Homer's heroes in their floppy figures. But these artists were not afraid to undertake battle scenes and have given us full-scale attacks from both sides, the Trojans attacking the Achaian wall (12) and the Achaians pursuing the Trojans, holding high the severed head of Ilioneus (14.495–500). They also continued the tradition of anachronism among Homer's illustrators. Since no one quite knew how Achaians and Trojans looked during the Bronze Age, it was standard to picture them in contemporary terms, which in the "Milan *Iliad*" means Roman soldiers fighting from horseback against a facade of Roman architecture. While the painters made some attempt to differentiate Achaians from Trojans (the former wear greaves, the latter leggings) and to mark gods with halos, their assumption is that Homer's readers can see themselves and their world in Homer's fictional universe.

The Middle Ages did not know the *Iliad* and the *Odyssey*. What they did know, apart from the Trojan materials mediated by Vergil and Ovid, were the pseudo-Homeric "Troy Stories," fantastic combinations and permutations of legends assembled by some very long-winded writers, notably Benoit de Sainte-Maure, whose influential *Roman de Troie* (1160–70) runs to six volumes in the standard modern edition. Like the "Milan *Iliad*," these compilations were often illuminated. Again, the illustrators favored crowded scenes of battle and the more spectacular events of the fall of Troy, and, again, the illustrations were anachronistic, with Homer's heroes turned into heavily armed knights fighting from splendidly caparisoned horses. While brooding in his tent, Achilleus plays chess, not the lyre, and Troy is a French city with Gothic palaces and churches. No matter. What the painters sacrificed in historical precision they gained in immediacy. Never again would the Bronze Age world of the poems be so close, so relevant, to the world of their readers.

Although the Renaissance rediscovered Homer, the difficulty of his Greek and the crudity of the earliest translations impeded his popularity. Painters and sculptors continued to find that Vergil gave a more circumstantial account of the fall of Troy than Homer did, and the taste of the time favored the loves of the gods as narrated by Ovid and interpreted by contemporary allegorists over the unvarnished exploits of Homer's heroes. The *Iliad*, with its inscrutable protagonist, offended contemporary readers, but the *Odyssey* could be allegorized into a proto-Christian homily of the wise man's progress through a stormy life to a heavenly salvation. This was probably the program behind the first great exposition of Homer in Renaissance art, when François I imported Italian culture into France in the shape of fifty-eight frescoes done around 1540 by Primaticcio and Nicolò dell'Abate for the "Gallery of Ulysses" at Fontainebleau (see Briganti; Zerner). These paintings, done very much in the elegantly contorted mannerist style, impressed Rubens and Poussin, but they were destroyed in 1737 when the gallery was torn down, and they exist today, apart from a few surviving versions, only in a 1633 series of drawings. A great loss, since they constituted the most prestigious record, done with great fidelity and detail, of the *Odyssey* in European art.

Somewhat later, Pellegrino Tibaldi (1527–96) painted a cycle of illusionistic ceiling frescoes for the Palazzo Poggi (now the Palazzo dell'Università) in Bologna. Here the style is even more exaggeratedly mannerist, as the familiar *Odyssey* figures strike bizarre and agitated poses in what has been described as a secular parody of the Sistine ceiling (Briganti 47). *Iliad* 5 and 17 received a similar treatment in 1537–39 by Giulio Romano and his assistants in the "Troy Room" of the Gonzaga palace in Mantua. Again, the program was allegorical—the fall of Troy seen as the defeat of Aphrodite, the victorious goddess in the judgment of Paris and the defender of the Trojans (Hartt 1: 181). Giulio Romano illustrated Diomedes's victory over Pandaros and his wounding of Aphrodite, a favorite incident for the allegorists, since it seemed to show the brave man's victory over the powers of passion.

But apart from these cycles, Homer was sparsely represented in art before the eighteenth century. Troy subjects had early appeared on tapestries, and Rubens did a series of oil sketches (1630–32) on the life of Achilleus, including the quarrel with Agamemnon (another favorite, since Athene's restraint of Achilleus could be allegorized as the victory of reason over wrath) and the surrender of Briseis, two subjects also painted later (1757) by Giambattista Tiepolo to decorate the Villa Valmarana near Vicenza (see Held). From the *Odyssey*, via Ovid, came an extraordinarily popular incident: Hephaistos's "netting" Ares and Aphrodite in bed together and inviting all the Olympians (the goddesses stayed home) to witness the blacksmith god's bitter triumph. Again, the scandal and comedy of this spectacle were redeemed by its moral, adultery duly punished, and by its allegorical message, that the artisan and artist must combine in their works both beauty and strength. Even so un-Homeric an artist as François Boucher, the court painter of eighteenth-century Versailles, could not resist this subject, creating a sumptuously rococo version of the couple's divine discomfiture. But neither the warfare of the *Iliad* nor the adventures of the *Odyssey* provided suitable subjects for the painters of politesse, particularly since their house goddess, Aphrodite, fares badly in Homer. She is successful only once, when she rescues her favorite, Paris, from Menelaos during the duel (3); the Worcester Art Museum has an oil sketch of this incident by Boucher, his only war subject.

It was in the reaction against the hedonism of rococo art and the painters' preoccupation with the prerevolutionary world of aristocratic privilege and frivolity that Homer experienced a resurgence of interest. In the "romantic classicism" of the late eighteenth and early nineteenth centuries, artists turned to the epic, particularly the *Iliad*, for subjects of moral earnestness and personal nobility (see Wiebenson). Alexander Pope's stately and vigorous translations inspired Gavin Hamilton to do a series of six *Iliad* paintings (1760–75) of muscular characters grouped in statuary poses, and the vases then being unearthed at Pompeii and Herculaneum offered painters models that approximated historical authenticity of detail and setting. Antonio Canova and Bertel Thorvaldsen, the best of the neoclassical sculptors, did Iliadic themes in this new and graver style. But most noteworthy were John Flaxman's illustrations (1787–94) done for both epics and often published with the Pope translations (Essick and La Belle). Flaxman's flat, friezelike engravings depict Homeric scenes in the severely linear fashion of Greek vase painting, a two-dimensional technique that does little to convey the color and spaciousness of the Homeric world and is especially inappropriate for the crowded violence of the *Iliad*'s war scenes. Some may also find Flaxman's unshaded designs thin and monotonous, but there is no doubt that his work was extraordinarily popular and caused something of a revolution in contemporary art history. For after the lushness of much rococo art, with its subjects drawn from the Roman world, here was a return to what many took as the purity, clarity, and simplicity of the Hellenic spirit. Not only did Flaxman's work seem to personify the ethical idealism of Greek antiquity, but his linearism seemed to express the very essence of art itself. Such ideals led other neoclassical painters to search out the Homeric characters and subjects that exemplified the high morality of antiquity. Angelika Kaufmann, Benjamin West, J. F. A. Tischbein, and Jacques David all turned to Andromache, particularly in her farewell to Hektor and in her grief over his death, as the model for the noble widow, the stoic victim of her husband's dutiful self-sacrifice (Rosenblum 39–42).

Less exalted was the Homeric world of Flaxman's contemporary, the Swissborn British painter Johann Heinrich Füssli (a.k.a. Henry Fuseli), whose nightmare paintings represent the darker side of the Romantic movement (Tomory). From the *Iliad* Fuseli did Achilleus grasping at the shade of Patroklos, cutting his hair over his friend's body, and lying in death himself. Four of Fuseli's most important *Odyssey* paintings depict Odysseus: one shows him as a small or dark foreground figure before the imposing Teiresias and a circular swirl of souls; in another he vainly brandishes a shield before the menace of Skylla; a third shows him about to be shipwrecked and accepting a veil from Ino/Leukothea; and in the last he is hiding under a ram that looks up at the shadowy, massive, and oddly pathetic bulk of a grieving Polyphemos. Another visionary was William Blake (see Raine), and although he did not illustrate Homer as he had Dante and Milton, his *Sea of Time and Space* (1821) is a curious montage of two Odyssean scenes, one of Odysseus shipwrecked on the shore of the Phaiakians and returning the veil given him for his safety by the sea goddess (5.458–60), and the other based on the cave of the nymphs (13.102–12), where Odysseus hides his possessions after the Phaiakians have landed him on the shore of Ithaka. Homer's Neoplatonist readers had seen in the cave, with its two entrances, an image of the world itself. In an elaborate explication Kathleen Raine (74–97) suggests that Blake pictured Odysseus as humanity delivered from the generative waters of life and putting off mortal garments (the veil), this cycle of life and death then repeated at the top, right, and bottom of the painting, where nymphs weave the purple webs. These webs represent the bodies we wear as we descend into the cave of this life, only, like Odysseus, to give them back to the gods as we emerge from the waters of time and reach our transcendent Ithaka.

A more personal symbolism appeared later in the nineteenth century in the Homeric canvases of Gustave Moreau (see Mathieu), whose paintings of a lonely Helen conveyed his obsession with the figure of the destructive woman. From the *Odyssey* he twice painted the Sirens, and one of his most distinctive works is a large, crowded, and unfinished canvas of the slaying of the suitors, with Odysseus reduced to a supporting role in a massacre dominated by an epiphany of Athene (Mathieu 45–46). Other painters of a symbolic persuasion generally found their inspiration in the archetypal world of the *Odyssey*. The Swiss Arnold Böcklin did a pillarlike Odysseus gazing mournfully across the ocean while Kalypso solaces herself with music before her cave, the contrast between pillar and cave presumably symbolizing the sexuality of their relationship. During World War II Max Beckmann found expression for his own sense of exile in the wandering Odysseus, who is represented once as he sailed past the Sirens and again when cared for by a solicitous Kalypso; while a 1931 Georges Braque drawing graphically contrasts Odysseus with Circe, the hero all straight and ascending lines, his temptress all x's and swirls. From the *Iliad* we have two versions by Giorgio De Chirico of Hektor and Andromache, the more famous 1917 painting suggesting the dehumanization of war by showing two mannequins embracing against the backdrop of an abstract and empty Troy.

More conventionally illustrative has been the work of popular British painters of the last hundred years—Hacker, Waterhouse, Etty, Burroughs, Linnell, Draper, and others. Of particular interest is Lord Leighton, who painted two of Homer's unhappy women: the Nausikaa, who must sadly watch Odysseus depart, and a black-clad Andromache, who must stand in line to draw water with other slave women, her fate the fulfillment of Hektor's gloomy prophecy of what happens to the wives of defeated soldiers (*Il.* 6.457; Ormond and Ormond, plates 5, 8). A greater painter than these, J. M. W. Turner, did an impressive canvas, often reproduced, of Odysseus jeering at a Polyphemos who is less a cannibalistic giant than a natural phenomenon, his cloudy head and shoulders looming over the tiny Odysseus. Across the channel the Ecole des Beaux-Arts in Paris set Homeric subjects twelve times in the first half of the nineteenth century for its annual Prix de Rome. Recently a number of the winning paintings have been reproduced in color in a handsome volume (Grunchec). Most of them are by such long-forgotten artists as Gustave Boulanger, Jean Alaux, and Léon Pallière, but in 1801

J.-A.-D. Ingres won first prize with a striking depiction of the embassy scene from *Iliad* 9. He later did a small jewel of a work, recalling Flaxman in its design, that shows Aphrodite wounded by Diomedes, but his most famous Homeric painting depicts the less familiar supplication of Zeus by Thetis (1.500–01), the flowing lines of her soft and boneless body appropriate for a sea goddess as she kneels before a magnificent deity modeled after Phidias's Olympian Zeus, touches him at the knee and chin, and, just for emphasis, nudges his toe with her own. Finally, to add a satirical footnote, there are the Daumier lithographs of a tubby Helen thumbing her nose at Menelaos and the reunion of a dowdy Penelope and a toothless Odysseus, both in the artist's "Ancient History" series (1842).

Meanwhile, illustrated editions have continued to appear wherever Homer is being translated, most recently by Leonard Baskin (Lattimore, *Iliad*) and by Hans Erni (Fitzgerald, *Odyssey*). Some may find the Baskin too patchy and the Erni too sketchy to compete with the expressiveness of a Greek vase painting or the animation of a Tibaldi fresco or the richness of a David canvas. None of the illustrators—with the exception of Flaxman—has achieved the status of, say, Doré for his work on Dante, and no contemporary painter has given the poems the attention of a Primaticcio, an Ingres, or a Moreau. A pity, for the experience of reading, which is temporal and discursive, can only be heightened by an analogous experience that is immediate and presentational. As for Homer, the diversity of his styles and scenes deserves periodic reinterpretation in the idiom of art, and his readers will always feel the need for the artist to bridge, with color and line, that mysterious space between the poems and their audience.

Teaching Homer in Honors Composition

George D. Economou

> The thought of what America,
> The thought of what America,
> The thought of what America would be like
> If the Classics had a wide circulation . . .
> > Oh well!
> > It troubles my sleep.
> > Ezra Pound, "Cantico del Sole"

The classics have kept circulating—if not widely, still in ways that might have surprised the poet who wrote the above lines. They have kept circulating with a persistence that indicates, perhaps, one of Pound's positive legacies: the need to return to and learn from the classics, particularly Homer, whose *Odyssey* Pound explicitly referred to in the beginning of his own epic *The Cantos*: "And then went down to the ship."

When in July 1983 I, myself, set out on a journey from New York City to Norman, Oklahoma, after a tenure of twenty-two years at the Brooklyn Center of Long Island University, to chair the English department at the University of Oklahoma, I thought about my first course in my new appointment. Wanting to learn the program and the student body from the bottom up, I had already requested a section of freshman composition, specifically one of five sections of honors composition regularly offered by the department in which qualified freshmen satisfy the university's two-term, six-credit composition requirement in one term of work. If my sense of duty dictated I start at the bottom, my sense of fun and new-found authority urged me to start with the best of that bottom. At some point during that interstate experience guided by Exxon and Holiday Inn signs, it came to me that the *Iliad* and the *Odyssey* should be the reading matter for the course. This sudden and unpremeditated decision—a natural for my very first class in a new place where I would be teaching students in their first, and for some, their only course in literature and writing—was an obviously symbolic as well as practical choice to begin with beginners at the beginning.

A medievalist by academic trade, I had, nonetheless, probably taught the Homeric epics more often than I had any other works of literature, with the exception of Chaucer's *Troilus* and *Canterbury Tales*. I had taught them in numerous lower- and upper-division courses, in an honors seminar, and once most profitably in a graduate seminar on the epic tradition. But I had never taught the *Iliad* and the *Odyssey* in a first-year English course, in which they were to provide the major subject matter for the types of themes we traditionally associate with freshman composition. If I had any doubts about the rightness of this decision, I had them about my own ability to ignite my unknown students' interest in Homer early in the course but never about the ultimate effect reading him would have. I knew Homer would, as always, come through, and he did.

When I first met my students, I learned that all of them had, of course, heard of Homer, a couple had read some of the *Odyssey*, but none had expected to have to read his two ancient poems in their composition class. Demonstrating their youthful flexibility and the resignation of entering freshmen, they seemed to tolerate my suggestion that the destiny of registration had involved them in a noble and unusually rewarding enterprise. My position from the start with my fifteen premed, prelaw, engineering, journalism, environmental design, business, and undecided majors was that to read Homer is not only an educational necessity but a special privilege as well and to think and write about his poems a unique pleasure.

The following account simply describes the plan of work for the semester without attempting to assess the effectiveness of any of the assignments. Some were more successful than others for the class as a whole, some for certain students rather than others, and some I would not repeat were I to give the course again. What we did in our thirty seventy-five-minute meetings was to divide the term into two seven-week units in which we read (usually three books per assignment), talked about, and wrote and revised —revised a lot—essays on the *Iliad* and the *Odyssey*. (I used Lattimore's *Iliad* and Fitzgerald's *Odyssey*, but the number of translations one can select from certainly attests to the strong currency of Homer's poems today.) Running throughout the semester was a journal assignment in which every student was required to write an entry of at least 250 words for each class meeting except for the first and last (the average entry, it turned out, would be much longer). These ungraded but absolutely required twenty-eight dated and numbered journal entries were mainly meant to provide regular writing practice, to anticipate some of the approaches and topics of the essay assignments, and to give the class specific issues on which to focus from one session to the next. Many a class discussion was launched by the reading of two or three journal entries for that day. The topics for these entries, which I describe in detail below, were sometimes announced at the beginning of a class for the following meeting, but just as often they were arrived at and formulated at the end of a period of discussion.

As the assignments in a one-semester composition course, the formal essays ran the gamut from a subjective paper to a short research paper and covered various kinds of expository, critical writing from character description to episode and theme analysis. The first essay followed the reading and discussion of Keats's "On First Looking into Chapman's Homer" at the beginning of the semester. Talking about Keats's poem not only introduced the class to rigorous close reading and some literary terms, it also served as an occasion to remark on the importance of Homer to past generations, a subject that was brought up in various ways throughout the semester. For the first journal entry, the class was asked to discuss the progression of metaphors and similes in Keats's sonnet and to pick the one that best expressed the young poet's "high." For the first theme, they were asked to describe an analogous personal experience, a "high" induced not by something ingested or inhaled but by something read, seen, or heard. Some responded with accounts of experiences involved in reading a novel or attending a rock concert, others with descriptions of experiences in the great outdoors or of moments of profound patriotic feeling. Stressing the need for fidelity to their memory of the experience in order to write about it responsibly and sincerely, which is to say in meaningful detail, I required thorough and sometimes complete revisions of these essays. By the time the initial round of conferences ended and the revisions were written, we were well into the *Iliad*, and the need to write responsibly about it, and later the *Odyssey*, became a paramount and constant concern. Other in- and out-of-class themes dealt with character description in the *Iliad*, the role of the Olympians, the changes Achilleus goes through, an important scene between two individuals of the opposite sex—mortal, immortal, or mixed—in the *Iliad* or the *Odyssey*, and a comparison-contrast of Achilleus and Odysseus. This last was first drafted as an at-home essay, and then, after correction and discussion of the nature of the assignment and the quality of students' performances in class and during individual conferences, it was revised into final form during the last meeting of the semester.

The short research paper required gathering information on one of several topics and then applying that information to an appreciation of the Homeric poems. The students wrote about every topic on my list: the wedding of Peleus and Thetis, the birth of Aphrodite, the birth of Athene, the Cyclopes, Teiresias, Zeus versus the Titans, the naming of Odysseus; and one student asked and was permitted to do research and write on the building of Troy. They were not only directed to use the staples on the reference library shelves but also encouraged to look into Hesiod's *Theogony*, the Homeric hymns, and Apollodorus's *Library* in the Loeb Classical Library edition, not so much for his accounts of the myths as for the value of being exposed to the superbly detailed annotations provided by Frazer, themselves among the best primary-source references on the subject of classical myth available. (I cannot resist sharing the witty title of one of the best of this set of papers, "There's More to Cyclops than Meets the Eye.")

While these formal writing tasks illustrate some of the more substantial and abiding concerns of the term's work, the journal assignments better reveal the daily character of that work. On a few occasions the students were free to choose their own journal topics, but most of the time they preferred to pursue the ones I selected. Several times early in the term we focused on isolating and describing the function of an unfamiliar convention in Homer. Later, when we were nearly finished with the *Odyssey*, some of these conventions, "epic digression" for example, were revisited. I also asked them to focus on a single social custom, on a detail or episode in which Homer betrayed a sense of humor, on a moment of extraordinary pathos, on any detail that struck them as unusually insightful into human nature. They wrote about Achilleus's shield and then about Auden's poem "The Shield of Achilles," which was distributed not only to vary our fare but also to reinforce the sense of Homer's lasting importance and to exemplify how poetry itself can be part of the creative process that produces new works of art. Similarly, we read and they wrote on Yeats's "Leda and the Swan" when we were considering the causes of the Trojan War. They wrote about the last scene of the *Iliad*, about Odysseus's first appearance in the *Odyssey*, and about his reunion with Agamemnon and Achilleus in Hades. They wrote about the image of women in the *Odyssey* and more than once about the recognition scenes in the second half of the poem, whose sequence, variety, and juxtaposition occupied us considerably, especially the question of the time of recognition of Odysseus by Penelope. But the high point of the journal assignments came with the term two-thirds over when the class divided into Achaians and Trojans; each student first wrote a defense of his or her nation's actions and then paired off with an antagonist for mutual refutation and rebuttal. These six-part "single combats," as we called them, enlivened our class hours and introduced the participants to the pleasures of debate and argument in a context in which they had equal knowledge and access to the same weapons. Naturally, some were superior fighters and delighted in going in for the rhetorical kill: "Agamemnon deserved rewards for leading us through the battle, and we felt honored to be part of it. It was our decision to go. He did not force us. We threw the first spear, but you Trojans threw the first insult." In an effort to bring our concern with the arts of persuasion up to date, we added one more assignment in the Achaian and Trojan personae, a script for a one-minute television commercial in behalf of their respective causes.

During the semester, my emphasis on the value of keeping the journal grew almost to equal that placed on the graded writing. As practice writing, journal entries played an important role in preparing students for the assignments on which their final grades would be largely based. But more important, keeping journals allowed them to write about Homer's poems regularly without worrying about grades, to connect with the poems' genius in ways more varied and personal than most formal writing assignments allow. The keeping of these journals, the backbone of the course, along with the other required papers has convinced me more than ever that reading and writing ought to be closely integrated and that the reading of great literature has a positive influence on the quality and even the quantity of writing students are willing to do. At our end-of-term conferences, most of my students were astonished at the amount of writing they had done, which lay there, in stacks two to three inches high, on the desk between us.

Because it was a course in composition, not classical literature or Homer, such things as authorship, oral poetics, and the epic tradition were introduced briefly but pointedly enough to impress the class that they would have to be seriously considered at a future, higher plateau of study. Similarly, there were moments when I had to choose between pursuing subjects directly related to the texts or to their influence on later literature and concentrating on aspects of our writing assignments. Usually I withstood the temptation to go literary and chose to distribute a number of opening paragraphs from student papers for group criticism instead of copies of Tennyson's "Ulysses" for group appreciation. However, I always made reference to such works on the board and urged the class to check them out for themselves. In my earlier teaching days, I would have found making this choice more difficult and probably would have believed that using the Homeric poems in a freshman composition course, even one on an honors level, would have intolerably restricted my teaching of them, would have cramped my style. Since those days, I have been learning that my work involves adapting my style to the work of literature and the work of the class rather than the other way around, especially in lower-division teaching. Now I am convinced that Homer suffers no indignities by serving as the reading for a composition class. In fact, his students and teacher came away the richer and his circulation a little wider.

Teaching Homer as History

Ronald P. Legon

As a historian, I may be regarded as an interloper among language and literature specialists, but I believe that my experience in teaching a freshman history course designed around Homer demonstrates that in history, too, "Homer will be all the books you need." For, in designing an alternative to the survey history course, I could find no topic in classical history as well suited as "the world of Homer."

The World of Homer, as I call my course, was an outgrowth of my dissatisfaction with the survey approach to introducing college students to history. In most humanities and social science disciplines, and in all the sciences, the student is exposed from the outset, not merely to the conclusions, but to the techniques and concerns of the discipline. Yet, in the typical history survey, the overriding emphasis is on the polished reconstruction of some great swath of the past. Source readings have, admittedly, become an essential element of such courses, but they are most often used to "illustrate" the main themes of the course or allow students an opportunity to express their personal reactions to vivid glimpses of a past era. When token attempts are made to deal with unresolved problems through ambiguous or contradictory source material, the student's typical reaction is bewilderment or panic. I have heard many students in such courses ask simply to be told "what really happened." They may learn the general outlines (as currently understood) of a major historical period but have only the vaguest notion of how historians developed that picture and the tentative basis on which many of its elements rest.

Can the freshman history student be made to understand what the business of investigating and writing history is about? I believe so, but to convey history to the novice as a process and as a series of techniques, one must abandon the primary purpose of the survey course—that is, sweeping coverage—in favor of an intensive examination of a small piece of the past. Ideally, the topic should be one that can be encompassed in a single term. In other words, it should be so circumscribed that, in a limited period of time, the student can become familiar with all the relevant documents in their entirety and a substantial proportion of the relevant background. With such a topic, students may be given a sense of discovering the facts for themselves by constructing and testing hypotheses and defending conclusions in research papers.

In the light of these criteria, the world of Homer seemed to me an ideal topic. This phrase, however, connotes a problem more than it does a description of a precise era of Greek history. Today the *Iliad* and the *Odyssey* are generally accepted as the final products of a long evolution of oral poetry. Some scholars place the beginnings of that poetic tradition in Mykenaian (Bronze Age) Greece, that is, the world in which the narrative themes of the two epics are set. Others see only the most tenuous links to the Mykenaian past and identify the poems as the products of the post-Mykenaian Dark Ages (11th and 10th centuries BC), which retained only a vague and distorted memory of the earlier era. The Dark Ages themselves stretched over more than three centuries during which there were dramatic changes in settlement patterns, material civilization, and so on. In any case, the epics did not assume their final shape until literacy established itself in Greece in the eighth and seventh centuries, BC, in the age of the emerging city-states. Historians also differ on the extent to which conditions during this final stage of the epics' gestation influenced their content and worldview.

For the historian interested in the development of Greek civilization in the critical half-millennium stretching from the last stages of Mykenaian culture through the Dark Ages to the establishment of the city-states, there are serious problems of evidence. The situation is well stated by G. S. Kirk in *Homer and the Epic*:

> [A]part from the Linear B inventories from Knossos, Pylos and My-cenae, the Homeric poems themselves, and a few Hittite and Egyptian references, there exists no contemporary record until the 7th century. Much of the reconstruction has to be founded on later mythological tradition, itself often derived from Homer, and on archaeological evidence—together, at one or two points, with the evidence of non-Greek proper names that survived into the historical age. All these kinds of evidence, particularly the first two, are erratic in scope and ambiguous in interpretation.   (33)

Yet, ironically, the very evidential situation that perpetuates uncertainty among professional historians creates an opportunity for the novice. Apart from the Homeric epics, the varieties of information identified by Kirk may be presented to the beginning student in compact and digestible form. To encompass effectively the major features of Mykenaian society derived from the entire corpus, Linear B documents can be chosen that resonate partic-ularly with features of the two epics. Archaic and classical Greek references to the Bronze Age and the Dark Ages, as well as to Homer, are brief enough to be read in their entirety. Finally, there are several excellent summaries of the archaeological evidence, including the appropriate chapters of Kirk's *Homer and the Epic* (3–5, 8), that can be assigned. Thus the preponderance of the student's effort and attention can be devoted to an intensive, critical reading of the *Iliad* and the *Odyssey*.

The poems are subjected to both external and internal criticism. Tom Jones's *Paths to the Ancient Past* gives good working definitions of both:

> The identification and authentication [of a document] involves a process called *external criticism*. The main questions to be answered are: What is it? Where did it come from? What is its date? Is it genuine? . . .
>
> "[I]nternal criticism" is applied to evaluate the evidence of sources of which the identity is known. A perfectly genuine document may be of little or no value for a variety of reasons: its author may have been . . . incurably biassed, lacking in perception, or just a plain liar. The question which internal criticism seeks to answer then is: "What is it worth?" (98–103)

Jones was not particularly thinking of works of dramatic or poetic fiction, but clearly the same principles apply to them as to historical narratives, diplomatic communiqués, and so on. But the investigator, whether a student or a professional historian, must be cognizant of the added difficulties of extracting facts from a fictional or at least highly embellished document. He or she must treat the work as itself an artifact of its time that unconsciously reveals many things never explicitly intended. The investigator must not be content to understand the author's purpose and message but must ferret out information whose presence the author was either entirely unaware of or had taken for granted as necessary but inconsequential background.

Thus, to take one example from so many, the emotionally charged meeting of Andromache and Hektor at the Skaian gates at the end of book 6 of the *Iliad* also provides evidence on a host of topics, from the ethos of the warrior class to the decoration of bronze helmets and from the position of women in Homeric society to notions of immortality and the meaning of life. Every episode is rich with layers of significance, once one is attuned to them, and even the delightful metaphors and similes that abound in the epics reveal important aspects of the poet's world.

This process of careful, critical reading of a source lies at the heart of my course. Several weeks of class time are devoted to examining the first two books of the *Iliad* and selected passages from the remainder of the *Iliad* and from the *Odyssey*. These sections are read and criticized line by line, with increasing student participation. Eventually, students comb through the complete epics in search of data relating to specific research topics. Later, each student presents and defends a single hypothesis, citing the key evidence collected. Since the entire class has read through the same body of material with great care, the discussions that follow these reports are both lively and informed. Finally, each student submits a paper on his or her topic, citing and critically examining all the evidence gathered from the epics and other relevant source material.

Some examples drawn from student papers illustrate their range, their use of Homeric evidence, and their occasional sophistication compared with freshman efforts in more conventional history courses. A painstaking collection of evidence is shown in the following excerpts from a paper on artisans in the Homeric world:

> Throughout his poems, Homer laces, between the struggle of the Achaians at Troy and the wanderings of Odysseus, a thread which weaves informative descriptions of the various types of skills and crafts that were practiced during his time. There were metalworkers, "smiths" who fashioned the weapons of war and the hardware of the home (*Il.* 5.60). When Homer mentions these metalworkers he gives the impression that some smiths specialized in working with bronze (*Il.* 4.187), while others specialized in working with gold (*Od.* 3.425). Construction and woodworking were done by the labor of "carpenters" (*Il.* 13.390), "shipwrights" (*Od.* 9.126), and "architects" (*Il.* 23.712); and even though Homer never explicitly tells us of stonemasons, he does refer to this craft when he describes the Olympian household of Zeus with its "smooth-stone cloister walks which Hephaistos had built" (*Il.* 20.11–12). No less essential, although seldom mentioned, were the "potters," who with clay and wheel produced the many jars and containers for domestic use (*Il.* 18.600). Other specialists were the "bowyer" (*Il.* 4.110) and the "chariot-maker" (*Il.* 4.485). Although Homer makes it quite evident that weaving was a fundamental handicraft, this skill was practiced entirely within the home, for it was women's work and throughout the *Iliad* we find "Helen in the chamber; she was weaving" (*Il.* 3.125); and in the *Odyssey*, Penelope who "everyday . . . kept weaving on the great loom" (*Od.* 2.104).

This paper goes on to describe the activities of four craftsmen mentioned by name in the epics: Laerkes the goldsmith (*Od.* 3.425–38), the Trojan shipwright Phereklos (*Il.* 5.59–64), Tychios the leather worker (*Il.* 7.219–23), and Ikmalios the carpenter (*Od.* 19.55–58). Scattered evidence about each of these crafts is assembled under discussions of the master craftsmen. The many craft skills of Hephaistos are also described, and the paper concludes with a well-chosen passage on the craftsmanship of Homer's consummate hero, Odysseus:

In the closing scenes of the *Odyssey* we learn of the Homeric Handiman—none other than "resourceful Odysseus." After having slain the suitors, he must convince his wife Penelope that indeed after twenty years he has returned. To do so, Odysseus tells her of the bedroom that he had built before he left. He tells her boastfully:

I worked on it and nobody else. The long-leaved bush of a wild olive grew inside the yard. Flourishing in bloom. It was thick as a pillar is. So I built the bedroom around it till I finished it with close fitted stones and roofed it well above. And I put portals on it, jointed and closely fitted. Then I cut off the crown of the long-leaved wild olive; chopping the stump from the root up I hewed it with the bronze ax well and skillfully, and straightened it with a line. When I had fashioned the bedpost I bored it with an auger. Starting with that, I hewed out a bed till I finished it, adorning it with gold and silver and ivory. And I stretched over it an oxhide thong shining with purple.   (23.189–204)

Thus Homer closed his brilliant image of the world as he knew and saw it—revealed in fantasy, but founded on fact.

The nuances in this excerpt from a paper on the military panoply and fighting tactics show careful examination of the evidence:

The war belt was a confusing article. It seems that it could be worn three different ways. The belt was worn under the corselet: "Iphidamas stabbed to the underneath of the corselet . . . but could not get through the bright war belt" (*Il.* 11.234–36). The woven war belt could also be worn over the corselet: "The bitter arrow was driven against the joining of the war belt and passed clean through the war belt elaborately woven; into the elaborately wrought corselet" (*Il.* 4.134–37). Some warriors just seemed to wear a war belt without a corselet: "Aias struck him beneath the war belt" (*Il.* 5.615); "his bright gear lying beside him, . . . shield . . . spear . . . helmet . . . and . . . the war belt" (*Il.* 10.75–77). In these passages there is no mention of a corselet.

Many papers, of course, deal with more abstruse topics, such as the beliefs and ideals of Homeric society. Here, a student grapples with the confusing relationship between fate and divine power in the epics. Having discussed the power of the gods and examined the "abstract" conception of fate (*moira*), he observes:

The question still remains, "What is the function of fate in the Homeric universe, and how does it relate to men and gods?" I like to view it this way. Consider each man's life in respect to a road map. Fate states that you were born at point A on the map, and in the span of your life you will travel to point B on the map. Anyone who has ever looked at a map can tell you that there are many ways to get from one place to another. This is where the gods fit in. They play a large role in saying how men will get to their destination. They say whether a man will take a smooth highway in life or if he'll take a bumpy road. It is up to them largely if a man will get to his fated point quickly or after a long time. Men to a much lesser degree can fill in the details of the journey. . . . this seems to imply that there exist three levels of reality in the Homeric universe: the abstract, the Olympian, and the earthly. There is proof of such a stratification in the works when the dying Patroklos says to the triumphant Hektor: "No, deadly destiny [*moira*], with the son of Leto [the god Apollo], has killed me and of men it was Euphorbos" (*Il.* 16.849–50). Thus Patroklos was killed on three different levels.

Clearly, there is room for disagreement and debate here. This very passage in the *Iliad* continues, "you [Hektor] are only my third slayer," thereby suggesting that destiny and Apollo were the first agency—somehow inseparable—and Euphorbos the second. But this paper accomplishes a great deal and convincingly demonstrates that the student has seriously confronted the evidence.

Another student working with the same problem took a somewhat different approach:

The position of Zeus with regard to fate is not entirely clear. He seems to portray the guardian of fate and fulfills that which is fated. Zeus weighs his balances, and those who weigh the heaviest are the losers. . . . It is not really Zeus' decision as to what will happen (*Il.* 8.69–70). Zeus weighs his balances four times in the *Iliad* to see what will be the outcome of the conflicts. Thus Zeus is forced to obey fate.

The weighing of the balances becomes a more personal symbol when it decides the conflict between Achilleus and Hektor. The balance weighs more heavily for Hektor, and this fate must be carried out, so death comes (22.209). Zeus is shown only to be the guardian of fate. Death is ruled by another power beyond Zeus' control, which he and all the gods must obey. Hera tells Achilleus: "We shall still keep you safe for this time, O hard Achilleus. And yet the day of your death is near, but it is not we who are to blame, but a great god and powerful Destiny" (19.408–10). It is apparent that when the time of death is near, the gods must step aside to allow death to happen. Hektor realizes this when he has been tricked by Athene (22.297–303). He realizes that Apollo and Zeus, who had favored him in the past, cannot save him now because his fate is overtaking him.

The differing viewpoints and insights that students develop in the process of writing these papers lead to a fruitful interchange of views in the later stages of the course. I have learned a great deal about Homer and his world from these discussions.

During the last weeks of the course, while working on their papers, students read selections from the works of M. I. Finley, Denys Page, and others to see what professional historians have been able to make of the same material with which they have been grappling. I find that by this time students are capable of appreciating the insights of historians in ways that would have been impossible without having gone through their own personal struggle with the documents. They can also see through the unsubstantiated generalization, the omission of significant but inconvenient evidence, and so forth. In other words, they have, in a few short weeks, become reasonably sophisticated about history as a process. It is an awareness that should contribute significantly to their development, whether or not they pursue formal historical studies any further.

TEACHING SPECIFIC EPICS

Teaching the *Iliad* in a Literature Survey Course

Mitzi M. Brunsdale

An apprehensive handful of sophomore English majors approaches our survey course in world literature each September, ready to bolt at the drop of a syllabus. More sinned against in American school systems than sinning intellectually on their own, most of these uneasy students will be teaching our children in less than four years, and hence they will be largely responsible for one more generation's grasp of the indispensable basis of democracy, the gift of literacy. In the challenging attempt to transform shaky sophomores into competent, perhaps even inspiring, teachers, I feel we must begin with Homer's *Iliad*.

As "our first poem which might well have been our last poem too" (Chesterton 81), the *Iliad* is the foundation of Western literature and the core of our secondary teacher preparation in English at this small state-supported college. Our English majors and minors typically study world literature for three quarters when they are sophomores. During the first quarter, we read portions of the *Iliad* in the Fitzgerald translation, Greek tragedy and comedy, the *Symposium*, the first six books of the *Aeneid*, Roman drama, and portions of the Old Testament.

The eleven classes we devote to the *Iliad* follow the informal lecture sequence suggested by Gilbert Highet in *The Art of Teaching*. In the first three sessions I introduce the quarter's plan of work, the concept of mythology and its evolution among the ancient Greeks, and the historical setting and events of the Trojan War, while the students read appropriate selections from Edith Hamilton's *Mythology*. I distribute a reserve list of books and articles from which I have drawn background for the lectures and for our close reading of the epic in class. I strongly encourage students to explore these items for their daily written assignments, one- or two-page essays treating a specific aspect of that day's reading. In the next seven meetings, we attempt to place books 1, 3, 6, 13, 16, 22, 23, and 24 each in the context of the entire *Iliad*. During the eleventh class, we discuss the epic as it relates to other literary forms, and we outline critical trends as well as current scholarly preoccupations.

To atone in part for my hubris in spending only eleven class periods on the *Iliad*, I choose a slightly different keynote for each year's work. Around this keynote, I gear reading and writing assignments, background materials for the lectures, and supplementary reading lists, providing a unified approach to the *Iliad* and ensuring that the work can be adequately handled in the short time available.

To refresh—or gain—their requisite acquaintance with Greek myth, our students read selections from Hamilton's *Mythology* for our second and third sessions. For discussion during the second one, they must also bring three different documented definitions of myth. I add D. H. Lawrence's view of myth as "an attempt to narrate a whole human experience, of which the purpose is too deep, going too deep in the blood and soul, for mental explanation or description" (296). Lawrence's definition suggests the creative tension between Apollo and Dionysos that provides insight not only into Homer's use of myth but also into the mythic elements of later literature, especially Greek· tragedy, in many respects the descendant of the *Iliad*. During the next class, we consider "historical myth" as described by Morford and Lenardon: "a level of emotional and spiritual truth that illuminates character and elucidates philosophy" (89). To extend Macleod's assessment of the *Iliad*, "Its humanity is firmly and deeply rooted in an awareness of human reality and suffering" (7), I stress the illustrative story of Atys, "one under the influence of Atē, goddess of doom," which isolates for study "the triumphant heights to which mortals may attain in the face of dreadful uncertainties or death" (Morford and Lenardon 78). This phenomenon is so powerfully portrayed in the *Iliad* that many commentators describe the poem as the Greek "literary bible of humanism," the position it holds in our overall program. The reading assignment for the third class also includes a brief overview of the Homeric period from *Backgrounds of European Literature* (Horton and Hopper 9–99). The students produce summaries drawn from Hamilton's account of the Trojan War—its dreadful uncertainties, its deaths, its human triumphs. Helpful lecture material appears in J. V. Luce's illustrated "Troy and the Trojan War" (*Homer* 121–39) and in K. W. Gransden's "Homer and the Epic."

In our seven sessions dealing with individual books of the *Iliad*, we consider the host of pedagogical opportunities the *Iliad* offers. Our primary goal, without which nothing else can be accomplished, is to see that students begin to read with understanding, sensitivity, and close attention to the text. They must also use their respectful reading to train themselves to write about the text with precision and logic in their daily assignments, which are graded, returned, and discussed in detail with each student outside class. Concurrently, even when dealing with a translation, we must convey not only the difficulties but also the benefits of the study of foreign languages and literatures; we must incorporate the historical perspective of the work into our reading of the text; and we must encourage our students to acquire and practice the rudiments of literary analysis. We need to work toward establishing the sense of community that the *Iliad* offers to those who experience it with respect and affection, so that the artist's message becomes apparent in the totality of the work, evincing its worth in its genuine relevance to the human condition.

Learning to read a literary text is the first prerequisite for teaching, since it presupposes and reinforces the habit of humility. Admitting ignorance (hardest, perhaps, to oneself), finding the necessary information, and using it accurately are aspects of scholarly integrity that I try to establish through the first essay assignment on the *Iliad*, a comparison, with textual references, of the personalities of Achilleus and Agamemnon as seen in book 1, "Quarrel, Oath, and Promise" (Fitzgerald's title). The *Iliad* poses significant intellectual challenges, because it requires students to locate unfamiliar meanings and mythological references, recognize them in various contexts, and integrate them into the multitude of images by which Homer communicates his perceptions. When Briseis is led from Achilleus's tent to Agamemnon's, for example, "loath to go" (23), Homer encapsulates the entire opening conflict of the *Iliad*, which more than that of any other epic, I believe, captures the youthful reader's attention: the infringement of honorable personal prerogative by unethically wielded authority. To demonstrate the complexity of the dramatic situation, however, I also bring in E. R. Dodds's postulation of *ate* as "a partial or temporary insanity" (*Greeks* 17) that blinds Agamemnon and causes him to provoke Achilleus's fatal anger.

Paradoxically, teachers must know their material intimately before they can present it with a simplicity that allows their students to approach it without trepidation and absorb it with delight. Traditional short essays on the reading selections from the *Iliad* help students frame their reflections on the text in a logical written form. Analyzing any of the objective characterizations in book 3, "Dueling for a Haunted Lady," allows our prospective teachers to explore the concept of fairness to an adversary that is vital to understanding not only Homer's world but much motivation in Western culture. Helen's domination by "immortal madness" (81), one of my favorite topics for this assignment, is particularly important, since it approaches *ate* by way of the problem of desire versus conscience, a theme of the *Iliad* that reverberates down through all the women of subsequent literature who are haunted by the fatally lovely shade of Helen.

By studying the nobler face of love that Homer unveils in book 6, "Interludes in Field and City," where Hektor takes leave of his wife and child forever, I try to help students largely without experience in another language and literature appreciate the complexities of translation and the importance of acquaintance with a foreign language. We compare Fitzgerald's translation of Hektor's farewell with other versions by Chapman, Pope, and the Victorian professor who occasioned Arnold's essay *On Translating Homer*. The intensity of the passage permits us to share in the certainty of Greek literature that Virginia Woolf identified as its unmistakable sense of meaning "just on the far side of language" (32). Book 6 also reflects what Woolf calls "the sadness at the back of life which they [the Greeks] do not attempt to mitigate" (39), a stern backdrop for the Greek tragedy that follows.

Our students must also learn how to use historical material in literary study. They analyze the verisimilitude of the events in book 13, "Assault on the Ships," by drawing on documented historical sources for Homeric weaponry and warfare. John Chadwick's *Mycenean World* is a helpful reference for seeking out Homeric tactics that illustrate the psychological attitudes evident in the text. The pace, vivid description, and even the naturalistic detail of this book all appeal strongly to youthful tastes nurtured on the rough-and-tumble of personal and televised athletic contests. A corollary to the experience of book 13 is the *Iliad*'s central attitude toward violence. Through Homer's acute contrasts of armed conflict and psychological portraiture, the *Iliad* focuses more on the futility of violence than other ancient works do.

I expect student essays to include practice in handling the basic tools of literary analysis. Book 16, "A Ship Fired, a Tide Turned," advances the recognition of larger structural devices than the allusions, Homeric similes, imagery, and historical references already discussed; this book demonstrates in particular the turning point of the epic and the dramatic irony with which Homer treats it. These elements seem more readily identifiable in the *Iliad* than in other classics because of Homer's clarity of presentation and the intense emotional involvement the work generates for most readers. Book 16 also allows the introduction of large-scale critical observations integral to seeing the epical forest as well as the individual splendor of its trees. We find these observations in the view Gilbert Murray presents of Homeric culture as preparation for Periclean humanism and his account of the *Iliad*'s use through the ages to teach the values of Western civilization.

Students need to assess the sense of shared cultural values the *Iliad* provides when they write the essay I assign with books 22 and 23, "Desolation before Troy" and "A Friend Consigned to Death," in which I ask them to defend or refute a critical statement that leads to a reading for the *Iliad* as a whole. One that has proved especially productive is Chesterton's acknowledgment of the championship of the underdog as a predominant characteristic of Western Christianity: "Hector grows greater as the ages pass . . . [anticipating] all the defeats through which our race and religion were to pass[,] . . . that survival of a hundred defeats that is [the race's] triumph" (81). The quintessential humanity of the men and women of the *Iliad* shows us at once what human beings are, what they ought to be, and what they can become.

To view the *Iliad* in toto, the essay assignment for book 24, "A Grace Given in Sorrow," asks students to support a general summary such as Macleod's: "The *Iliad* is great not least because it can speak authentically for pity or kindness without showing them victorious in life" (16). This essay brings us full circle, requiring use of all the literary techniques learned thus far in the course; even more important, it asks students to look beyond these techniques to the greater stature of the *Iliad* as a comment on the human situation. One of Homer's mightiest images, for example, is Hecuba's reproach to Priam, "Iron must be the heart within you," and its echo on Achilleus's lips as he accepts Priam's supplication. In this masterstroke, as compact in utterance as it is gigantic in significance, Homer transcends even historical perspective and cultural community to achieve an eternal portrayal of compassion that binds together all who come to love the *Iliad* and its celebration of the best in humankind.

Our linked critical essays on the *Iliad* provide the best exposure I have yet found to fundamental literary techniques, allowing our students to approach the *Iliad* thoroughly enough to begin to love it. Highet's sound teaching model promises a workable plan for those early years when young teachers tend to teach as they themselves were taught; it may also provide a safe springboard for more mature teaching. By the close of our year of world literature, as we work through Arnold's vision of a cultural pendulum in "Hebraism and Hellenism" (Culler 465–75) and Frye's classifications of literature from *The Anatomy of Criticism*, our students invariably choose the *Iliad* as the standard for measuring other works and place the *Iliad* first on the model syllabi they draw up as a part of their final term projects.

I always approach the *Iliad* with a sense of inadequacy; I am not a classicist, and our students must work within the strictures of education degrees, not the more rigorous tradition of the liberal arts. But I can say this for them and for myself: we love the *Iliad*, and that love, I believe, enables us to teach it adequately at our respective levels, for Homer has shown us "what human character can be; what men and women have to do and to bear, how great they can be; life means more, is better worth living, when one has got Homer written in one's heart" (Glover 84).

Homer as the Door to Critical Theory

Sally MacEwen

Because Homer's work represents the beginning of a literary history, it provides a unique opportunity to examine the meaning of writing and literature. In my year-long survey course on ancient civilization, I use the *Iliad* not only to introduce the themes of Greek literature but also to study the way in which all words and written things may be considered. Given the level of the course, my primary goal is to introduce these questions in the hope that students will continue to examine them in their future readings in all courses. We do not pursue in depth what could be considered advanced philosophical reading or analysis of criticism. Three general questions are examined: the historical phenomenon of writing, the significance of style, and the power of "writing" itself.

The Historical Context

I begin the section of the course on Homer with study of the Dark Ages (c. 1200–800 BC), because I think it is important for students to attach the ideas of creating and writing to a real setting and a real poet before they address the more theoretical problems. First, the class tries to imagine the situation of the period (drawing on Kirk, *The Songs of Homer*, and using Page, *History and the Homeric* Iliad, for comparison); they discuss the realities of a life of hand-to-mouth agricultural existence, the perception of culture in such a time, attitudes toward the past, and, from these, the need for the creation of a "heroic" mythology. Students picture those who spend their workdays struggling to survive and their leisure time listening to storytellers at night or at festivals; then they imagine how the story and the interests of the listeners might interrelate. Next, they turn to the storyteller, the creative element personified, using the researches of Milman Parry among the Yugoslav oral poets (see Lord, *Singer*). At this point, they begin to move to the theoretical levels. The Yugoslav poet had a completely different attitude toward the "song" and the "story" (Lord, ch. 5). Students are always startled to realize that an oral poet describes as being the "same" two oral poems in which the plot is the same but the words differ. They soon see, however, that without writing, there is no "same" in our sense, especially given the mechanics of oral poetry and memorization.

The simplicity, even "innocence," of this stage in the history of literature quickly leads the class into deeper questions about literature and thought. Students see that one would consider words very differently if one did not have writing, for one could not check usages or accuracy in the same way. Two problems arise from this discussion: first, the definition of literature, and, second, the difference between fictional and historical truth. These lead to an even deeper problem, namely, the relation between language and thought.

When the class begins to discuss whether literature is only written and what the definition of literature is, it is also beginning to use different methods of criticism. Because Homer's predecessors are unknown, students cannot place the work in a traditional context or know what is "original." This uncertainty forces them to examine how much one needs to know about a literary tradition or even about an author in order to interpret a work, that is, to examine the question of "closed" or "open" text. Again, because of the formulaic nature of Homer's language, one can also discuss what makes the epic "original" and eventually approach several contextual techniques, namely, how to decide what weight of meaning to put on formulas, ring composition, and so on. (I expand on this topic later.) Finally, Homer's use of myth as fictional writing leads to definitions of myth and to a consideration of structuralist theory.

The question of historical truth vis-à-vis the Trojan War introduces methods of record keeping such as myth, rhetoric, and memory, as well as theories of historiography that I use later in the course. I find my students sometimes equate "myth" with falsehood (as in "That myth has now been disproved by science"), and so the first goal is to consider the existence of a transcendent sort of truth about the past and where it comes from in the creative process. Next, one realizes that the rhetoric of presentation has a great deal to do with the audience's perception of truth. Homer himself points out the importance of rhetoric and persuasion, especially with regard to Odysseus; for example:

> Odysseus, we as we look upon you do not imagine
> that you are a deceptive or thievish man, the sort
>   that the black earth
> breeds in great numbers, people who wander
>   widely, making up
> lying stories, from which no one could learn
>   anything. You have
> a grace upon your words, and there is sound sense
>   within them,
> and expertly, as a singer would do, you have told the
>   story. (*Od.* 11.363–69; trans. Lattimore)

Yet we know how well Odysseus can lie and thieve—the "grace" of his words and their poetic sound are what make them seem true. (Gregory Nagy in

The Best of the Achaeans shows this poetic grace to be equal in *arete* to battle prowess.)

That the storytelling quality is proof of the story's veracity seems odd at first to students raised on a sense of scientific objectivity, but they quickly see that they too may judge the truth of a statement by its rhetorical presentation. (Note Thersites at *Il.* 2.243–77, whose bad manners lead his listeners to reject his message when it is actually true.) What is more, oral poets actually think of themselves as historians (e.g., Demodokos in *Od.* 8, who does not differentiate between the "true" story of the Trojan War and the "myth" of Aphrodite), blurring the lines between true and false even more. The class begins to realize that even today the motives for storytelling and history telling may not be so different from each other. This topic is pursued later with regard to the historians who claim objectivity but feel no compunction about adding fictional elements in the name of "probability."

The questions of truth and probability in narrative lead to those of style and its impact and the relation between word and thought. In Homer, the interplay of words, ideas, and rhetorical impact presents itself with a sort of innocence, free from the self-consciousness of a literary tradition, because, in fact, there can be no tradition without writing. After Homer, the critic must consider the historical references of words, images, and themes through the study of past literature and other uses of specific words; in Homer, one may see simply the writer and his tools. He has learned poetry as a craft, so the words are for him tools, a means of continuing his tradition rather than changing it. (In one sense, of course, Homer is more tradition-bound than a writing poet, because, for example, he cannot call Agamemnon "swift-footed." This economy does not add complications to interpreting his words, however, because the words have no added layers from the tradition.)

When Homer begins a story, newness is not an issue, yet he nevertheless creates a unique piece of literature. First-time readers note especially the concreteness of his language and description, but he creates his unique effects from choices taken from traditional words and phrases. Homer's words do not contain layers of meanings in themselves (by being concrete and abstract) or in their tradition; instead, the tension of multiple meanings in his poetry comes entirely from his juxtapositions and arrangements of formulas, set scenes, and so on (see Vivante, *Epithets*, for examples). Writing poets also use arrangement, but a reader must consider many other aspects of their work. In Homer, one has easy access to the message because the messengers are so much simpler than those of literary works with a written tradition behind them. When Homer makes a choice, it is more transparently visible partly because it is different from our set of choices and partly because all his choices are available for our analysis. Nevertheless, he has a great number of choices in formulas and epithets, in speeches and similes, in divine interventions, in parataxis and ring composition, and in his myth.

Using our picture of Homer facing "writing" for the first time (a revised version of the Homeric question—see Kirk, *Songs*, pt. 5), we may examine artistic choice. Given his tools, what are Homer's choices, and if he had our choices, would he take them? The methods of contextualism come into play in force, because the significance of the words can only be found within the text. What is more, one must ask, if one cannot cross-check the occurrences of words in a concordance, can a formula signify at all in its individual words? Since the writer cannot be known, one must ask about the necessity of identifying "artistic intent" and what that intent means for interpretation. We have in Homer a truly self-defining context simply because of the circumstances, but the idea of "closed object" then appears for discussion. Once we realize how many layers later tradition adds, we must decide again what "writing" does for context, as well as vice versa. With these considerations, the class begins to analyze the text and to examine its own suppositions about analysis.

The limitations and potential of the study of Homer are now clear to the class: because Homer's vocabulary choices are made from a fairly rigid set of formulas and epithets and their position is determined by meter, the choices can all be gathered together and considered. For example, we can collect all Homer's epithets for a character, or all his descriptions of death in battle, and see exactly when he uses them. This leads to a consideration of the constraints on Homer's style and meter and how he uses or overcomes them. (For examples, see Fenik, *Typical*; Austin, *Archery*; Hainsworth, *Flexibility*; and Vivante, *Epithets*.) That Homer calls only Achilleus "swift-footed," for example, and only in a certain metrical situation, may mean he had no choice and therefore the actual signification of the epithet is null (swift-footed Achilleus = Achilleus), or it may show that Homer had means of manipulating formulas in the line so that he could use the formula or epithet of choice. One must then also ask if Homer has power or would want power over his choice of words. What is more, the critic who says "It's just an epithet" must show the basis for deciding which epithets are significant.

Once students recognize Homer's peculiar "closed set" of choices, they can see how choices might be made by authors of many periods. When they move on to the question of whether the occurrences of the epithet "swift-footed" are meant to recall one another, moreover, they must ask how this deliberate recollection could happen in an oral poem recited over many hours or days and how much the poet is aware of the repetition—another entry into the definition of closed or open text and context. Similarly, in comparing descriptions of an action such as death in battle, they can look at all the types and see when they are used ("a mist of darkness closed over both eyes" or "destiny closed over him" or more graphic descriptions).

The class turns again to Homer and his audience and discusses affect, for when Homer needs to make a particular point, he has only the tools of repetition and expansion. The students may also think about whether the critic should consider the impact on the audience at all—again closed or open context. The most obvious and perhaps most fruitful example is a comparison of the deaths of Sarpedon and Patroklos (both in *Il.* 16) and of Hektor (*Il.* 22). While many elements appear elsewhere (mourning gods, rolling helmets, order of throws, fainting), the number of elements and their arrangement indicate that these deaths are turning points and signify what is important about each death (Sarpedon's relation to Zeus, Patroklos's hubris and nemesis, Hektor's pathos). Because Homer does not or cannot give meaning abstractly, the choices within formulas and set scenes, or their verbatim repetition, create in the audience an impression of meaning. With a more modern style, Homer could tell us of deeper meanings and feelings, but he would also lose his unique impact. The clarity of his choices makes the student realize the effect of any choice in vocabulary and style. Thus the introduction of writing to literature leads us to understand the roots of style.

The Significance of Style

Study of Homer's concrete language shows how many ways a writer can say the same thing. While a modern writer has many methods for describing character, Homer's methods are strictly external—action and speech, again each with its own sort of impact. Not only individual characters but entire scenes or groups can be described by similes. On the next level of meaning, the subconscious and the superhuman cosmos appear in concrete guise as gods and their meddling. The workings of history and cause and effect in Homer's cosmos can be understood through an examination of parataxis and ring composition. Obviously the mode of presentation and mode of thought are closely related; eventually one must examine whether thinking, speaking, or writing is prior.

Speeches of Homer's characters provide an excellent means for reading behind language to find the relation between words and meaning. Here one evaluates the tools of externalization. Several examples appear in the opening scene of the *Iliad* at the conference of the Achaians concerning the plague (1.57–305): the speeches of Achilleus, Kalchas, and Agamemnon show internal feelings through external expressions and reactions (e.g., Kalchas's appeal to Achilleus shows Kalchas's fear and helplessness before the tyranny of Agamemnon; Achilleus's response shows the kindly side of his heroism). It is my purpose here not to analyze the passage but to tell how I use it in class, where students realize how externalization can take the place of description. They see that, like an abstract or descriptive style, the style that uses such concrete methods has virtues and a consistency of its own.

To study the similes, the class examines the opening of book 3, where the Trojans, likened to cranes, are contrasted with the prosaic but valorous Achaians (1–9). This simile is immediately followed by three more, about the physical appearance of the scene, of Menelaos, and of Paris—a rare grouping of similes. The possibility of multilevel analysis leads to discussion on how to read a simile. By recalling Homer's choice of tools and apparent simplicity of thought, one can consider how a simile works, whether concrete can signify abstract, and especially whether the abstract of, say, "disorganization in the Trojan ranks" exists if there are not the words to say it. And if it does exist, how can the simile create the same idea in the audience's subconscious and conscious? That the images work so well on so many levels belies the notion that Homer only thinks concretely; on the other hand, his limited vocabulary could imply limited thought. (For such an argument, see Snell, esp. ch. 1.)

The device of divine intervention involves another aspect of Homer's style that helps the class understand how writing works. While the device is not, strictly speaking, a necessity of oral poetry, it is nevertheless one of Homer's most effective uses of concrete for abstract. Once students realize that Athene's intervention at *Iliad* 1.193 is to be taken as something other than a literal event, they see that one can turn to other topics, such as how the intervention explains the event, how the audience knows this, and how modern writing expresses similar ideas.

The phenomena of parataxis and ring composition illustrate how language and thought affect each other. One must realize, first, that cause and effect are important in any narrative, historical and fictional, and, second, that the mode of expression can determine the analysis just as the mode of analysis can determine interpretation of the expression. When Homer, as a historian or as a poet, correlates events, his use of *post hoc, ergo propter hoc* parataxis may indicate that he has only the one mode of conception (see Hainsworth, *Flexibility*; Austin, *Archery*). But it might also indicate some "trace" of understanding of aetiology that cannot be stated. On the other hand, Homer uses ring composition to locate secondary information that is required in an order other than chronological. Not only does he have few subordinating conjunctions, but his thinking about events in order is very simplistic. He must recognize, nevertheless, that he cannot always consider events in their chronological order, that sometimes he must bring in background or other information out of order; he therefore employs in that situation the device of ring composition. One then must ask whether this device shows Homer can think synchronically and how we can analyze such a question. Obviously, we do not answer these questions in a survey course, but students, often for the first time, realize that one must examine thought and speech to know how to interpret any piece of writing, poetic or expository.

The Power of Writing

Finally, Homer's artistic choices regarding myth illustrate how the piece of writing takes on its own identity, separate from the author. When Aristotle compares the use of the myth of Achilleus in the *Iliad* to the use of myth in the average epic and pronounces the poem's greatness to be in its unity (*Poetics* 1451a), one sees perhaps the first expression of the critical presumption that the act of creation is generated by a structuring principle. Homer had many choices concerning where to stop and start the story of Achilleus and what parts to emphasize. Having read the *Iliad*, one sees how many small choices make a perfect whole (e.g., the placement of Achilleus's tragic choice at 1.417–18 and all the levels this choice entails, or the repression of his effort to avoid going to war). But one need not stop with the contextual description of all Homer's small choices; one can also consider the psychological or cultural source of this unifying principle and whether the unity feels equally correct to all readers, all writers, all cultures and periods; what makes it seem so obvious that proper structure has been followed or violated; whether all the elements—epithets, formulas, similes, and so on—create the structuring principle of unity or vice versa; and, finally, whether one can speak of a transcendent "structuring principle" at all.

When students see that choices create the structuring principle as well as vice versa, they can begin to consider what writing is in the ontological, even grammatological, sense. After observing the complexity of meanings in the poem, students realize how many abstract ideas are expressed with concrete vocabulary and images. Then they ask how the reader's mind makes connections between any idea and expression. But how do we know how to draw meaning from literary writing? Because we bring to the act of reading the assumption that writing will entail making such connections. Yet this is not the assumption of oral poetry necessarily or, more specifically, of storytelling. At some point, when stylus was set to wax, the "self-consciousness" of poetry was created, poetry that, in fact, set out to contrive an artifact rather than tell a "truth." It is not far from this point to ask what is the nature of such a truth, a topic clearly too complex for a survey course but one that I hope students will continue to examine in further studies.

What the *Iliad* Might Be Like

George E. Dimock

According to Dorothy Walsh, the essential function of literature is to convey what a given human experience might be like. From this point of view the *Iliad* not only tells us what happened as a result of the anger of Achilleus; it makes us feel in a particular way what that whole complex of actions "was like." We listen to Homer because he awakes in us a complicated emotional awareness that we cherish and could never have experienced unassisted. It follows that our duty as teachers of the *Iliad* and the *Odyssey* is to make these feelings as accessible as possible to our students. It is not enough for us to tell them what they ought to feel; they must feel Homer for themselves.

The best method I have found for getting students to read Homer on their own with sympathy and understanding is simply a version of explication de texte. Following the practice of Howard Porter and others who taught classical civilization at Yale in the late forties and early fifties, I encourage my students to comment in class on the work before them line by line and image by image, describing what the words convey. Even in translation this procedure can be surprisingly effective. Good translators do, after all, translate.

By way of example I hazard here a comment on the first seven lines of Lattimore's translation of the *Iliad*:

> Sing, goddess, the anger of Peleus' son Achilleus
> and its devastation, which put pains thousandfold upon the Achaians,
> hurled in their multitudes to the house of Hades strong souls
> of heroes, but gave their bodies to be the delicate feasting
> of dogs, of all birds, and the will of Zeus was accomplished
> since that time when first there stood in division of conflict
> Atreus' son the lord of men and brilliant Achilleus.

The feeling of desolation is unmistakable, unrelieved except for the epithet "brilliant" applied to Achilleus at the passage's end. The meter emphasizes the word "devastation," whereupon we hear how much Achilleus's anger injured his friends. Even if only subliminally pronounced, the four heavy aspirates in the phrase "hurled in their multitudes to the house of Hades strong souls / of heroes" make us experience physically the hurling forth of the breath-soul. The thought ends with the sickening image "of dogs, of all birds" toying with the corpses of so many courageous slain—all this by the will of Zeus. With the keynote of desolation now established, the last two lines adumbrate the beginning of Achilleus's anger and tell the Muse at what point in the story Homer wishes her to begin. In doing so, they suggest the poem's essential conflict, that between Agamemnon's world of human limitation and the claims of the hero's divine brilliance. So Homer seems to characterize the entirety of the song he wishes the Muse to sing through him: how Achilleus's anger produced utter desolation and how Zeus wanted it that way. Are we as readers, we may ask our students, to prepare ourselves for fifteen thousand lines of unrelieved pain, or will Achilleus's brilliance somehow prevail in spite of it?

This, I think, is the kind of analysis we get if we ask ourselves what a passage conveys. If our feeling about the opening lines is correct, the *Iliad* will turn out to be an exhibition not so much of Achilleus's tragic flaw (*hamartia*) as of how his best efforts to assert himself as a hero ended in desolation through the will of Zeus. It is Achilleus's anger, not his *hamartia*, that the Muse is asked to sing, almost as though to celebrate it, and it is Zeus more than Achilleus who seems to be blamed for the disasters it causes.

At the end of this paper I suggest how the scene between Achilleus and Priam in book 24 supports an emphasis on Zeus's responsibility and at the same time transcends the desolation we have detected, but first I should like to indicate some further ways in which the *Iliad*'s invocation may serve to bring students into sympathy with the poem. From the very outset, I would urge them to take nothing for granted or as conventional. For example, when at the beginning of the first work of Western literature the poet asks a goddess to use him as her mouthpiece for the song we are about to hear, surely we should try to imagine how such a conception could arise. Anyone who has read the first book of the *Iliad* can see that the gods are thought of as putting things into people's minds from time to time, for we are told there that Hera put it into Achilleus's mind to call the fatal assembly. From this beginning a student can reasonably conclude that Homer and his contemporaries felt the coming to mind of especially good or crucial ideas as the invisible operation of one or another deity. Similarly, when poetically inclined individuals felt lines of poetry they had heard come unbidden to their lips, that impulse too might easily be imputed to divine agency. If we add to this picture a page or two (21–23) of Albert Lord's *Singer of Tales*, we and our students will have a basis for understanding how an impressionable young person who has been listening from infancy to the local style of narrative song first finds himself singing snatches to his sheep on the hillside and later whole songs to the people at home. As confidence grows and repertoire increases, he will probably become more and more aware of two things: of how stupidly and inconsistently less gifted singers repeat the old stories and of how powerfully the conviction imposes itself on his own mind that this way and not that one is the way the song should go. Carried away by the reality of the song as it presents itself to him in performance or practice and now able to think in the traditional poetic language, he will produce within the traditional framework speeches, scenes, and actions never heard sung before. Such a method of composition will cause a singer who believes in the gods no doubts about the song's authenticity. The enthusiasm, the spontaneously occurring poetic language, the vivid, immediate new images, all seem to come from god, from the Muses. What ordinary mortals remember of the past is a mere nothing by comparison. Homer says so himself as he prepares to sing the catalog of ships in the *Iliad's* second book: "for you are goddesses, are present, and know everything, / while we hear only the fame of it, and know nothing" (485–86; trans. mine). The singer literally feels the past become present in his mind, and who can blame him for believing that goddesses are making him their mouthpiece? Homer knew that poets often learn their songs from other poets, but he believed that the best singing comes directly from the Muses. I quote Phemios in book 22 of the *Odyssey* as he begs Odysseus for his life: "I am self-taught, and the god implants in me / songs of all sorts. Be sure I shall sing for you / as for a god . . ." (347–49; trans. mine). We know that Phemios cannot really have been "self-taught," but that does not prevent him, and others, from believing that his singing, both content and technique, comes exclusively from his own mind, planted there by divine influence.

Such an explanation of belief in the Muses can help our students accept the Homeric gods in general as neither fanciful nor arbitrary but, rather, as perceived in the first instance in phenomena that we ourselves consider real: the Muses are perceived in poetic inspiration, Aphrodite in falling in love, Poseidon in earthquakes, Zeus in thunderstorms, Ares in the stress of battle. All these phenomena suggest agencies beyond human control with a will of their own. How natural, then, for Homer's forebears to have endowed these agencies with personalities and the power of assuming, on occasion, quasi-human forms. As students become more familiar with this way of thinking, they will feel no undue surprise even when Strife, or Hate, as Lattimore translates her, ascends the deck of Odysseus's ship and cries out to both flanks of the Greek army as the poem's greatest battle begins. Like love or poetic inspiration, strife seems to transcend the purposes of the humans involved in it and to behave with a will of its own. Actually, most if not all of the nouns in Homer that we might be tempted to call abstract have enough personality to be available as gods or goddesses. Fear, Panic Flight, Sleep, and Death, like Strife, all call for capital letters on occasion as personified beings, divine in that, among other things, they are timeless and immortal. Achilleus may wish in *Iliad* 18.107 that Strife might perish from among gods and men, but she will not: she is "sister of Ares" and a permanent feature of the Homeric environment (4.441).

Once students perceive how broad the range of Homeric divinity is, they can easily be dissuaded from looking to Homer's gods for any strong moral imperative. They will be content to see them, in my colleague Kenneth Connelly's phrase, as gods of the world as it is rather than as it ought to be. Thus Homer's picture of events as the product of a large number of conflicting wills, divine and human, can be seen to accord with the world as we and our students experience it.

In spite of this apparent disunity, it is clear throughout the *Iliad* that the power of Zeus is supreme. As we have seen, the invocation ascribes the poem's outcome to his will, and at various points Zeus himself emphasizes that, as wielder of incomparable physical force, he can have his way whenever he wants it. As Lattimore points out, he can even save Sarpedon from his "fated" death; he merely chooses not to (16.431–61). He chooses not to, apparently, in order not to disturb what he and the other gods have accepted as being in the cards already. As Hera's speech suggests, if he does disturb what is fated, there will be no consensus left on Olympos at all—not an impossible situation, but an unpleasant one for Zeus as well as the others.

In other words the gods, Zeus included, accept the world as it is because they are unable to agree on anything better. At the same time, the course of events is manifestly the will of the gods, especially of Zeus, since if it were not, they or he would change it. We were right, therefore, when at the poem's fifth line we felt the words "and the will of Zeus was accomplished" to be something like a cry of protest. The invocation seems to say that this is a world in which the supreme striving of even the greatest of heroes may produce only a battlefield strewn with corpses. How can Zeus permit such futility?

As the poem unfolds, students will become aware that the heroes themselves expect fame and honor to be a sufficient recompense for their deaths. Just as plainly, Agamemnon's treatment of Achilleus suggests that they are not. Even when Agamemnon feels forced to offer Achilleus an unparalleled quantity of gifts to return to the fighting, it is obvious that he has no feeling of what the life of an Achilleus is really worth. He values the services Achilleus can offer, not what Achilleus is. This being so, where, and how, we may ask our students, is Achilleus to receive the honor his mother predicts for him if he returns to the fighting and dies?

When our classes finish reading the *Iliad*, I hope they will feel that Achilleus has won the honor due him. If anywhere, this happens in the ransoming of Hektor in book 24. There, after Priam and Achilleus have eaten together, they gaze on each other with wonder, and we should ask what it is they wonder at. What do they see beneath the good looks and admirable discourse named by Homer? Clearly, each deeply appreciates what the other has just done, and each understands, as far as is possible for another, all that it means. Each has experienced the other's greatest act of heroism and marvels at his worth. This is honor for both, and particularly for Achilleus.

Honor is recognition of worth. Priam honors Achilleus for giving him back the body of his son. Achilleus honors Priam for having kissed his hands, "the hands / that were dangerous and manslaughtering and had killed so many / of his sons" (478–80; trans. Lattimore). How is the worth of these two men conveyed by these actions? At the moment that Priam kissed Achilleus's hands, his gesture meant, "I love my son so much that, to get his body back, I can bear to kiss the hands that killed him." This is already much, as Achilleus recognizes, but Priam's full worth does not emerge until the gesture has come to mean, "In you I embrace the death of my son. I recognize that everything we cherish perishes and only the gods are happy, but I can find enough love to live even so." Considering what we have come to feel Hektor means to Priam, this is heroism indeed.

Achilleus's even greater worth is shown in that it is he who helps Priam to this higher heroism after finding the way to it himself. When at Zeus's and Thetis's urging he consents to allow Hektor's body to be ransomed, we cannot tell whether there is anything more in his mind than despair of making up for Patroklos's loss; but when Priam enters his hut, there is a hint that Achilleus has achieved a deeper acceptance: he has just eaten, a thing he had found impossible before Thetis came to him. Similarly, Priam becomes able to eat again when he finally accepts Hektor's death. We learn the nature of Achilleus's acceptance from his first words to Priam. Recognizing a fellow sufferer and admiring his courage, he tries to comfort him by sharing the acceptance he himself has achieved. It is indeed a terrifying recognition: only the gods are happy; humans are condemned to live in sorrow. To some, like Peleus and Priam, Zeus awards evil mixed with good; some (and here Achilleus evidently means himself) receive only evil. Zeus "makes such a man an object of insult; / an unbearable craving drives him over the face of the earth / and he goes honored neither by gods nor mortals" (531–33; trans. mine). Priam's son being dead by the dispensation of Zeus, grieving will not raise him up again. "Come," Achilleus says to Priam, "sit on a chair, and let us in spite of all / let our sorrows lie still in our hearts, though we feel them" (522–23; trans. mine).

It is a terrible acceptance Achilleus has achieved, and Priam is not yet up to it. He begs Achilleus not to make him sit before he sees his son's body, and he wants the ransom to be performed at once. Like Achilleus when he was dragging Hektor's corpse, Priam is still under the illusion that some action of his, taking his son's body back to Troy perhaps, can assuage his grief. At this failure to understand, Achilleus becomes very angry. Among other things, it is terrible to see someone else still suffering under the illusion one has oneself just discarded with such pain. In his anger Achilleus points out the true extent of mortal helplessness and the power of Zeus: Priam's supplication, brave as it was, is not what brought about the ransom of his son; Achilleus himself had already determined on it at the instance of his mother and Zeus. Nor would Priam be inside his shelter in the Greek camp without the gods' intervention. Priam must realize, Achilleus implies, that there is no human achievement whatsoever unless Zeus allows it. As it is, Priam's innocent hubris tempts Achilleus to do him violence.

At this outburst Priam naturally enough obeys and sits down. Whether he understands yet or not, Achilleus's anger has disposed him to be instructed, and his submission in turn allows Achilleus to carry out his original generous intent. Priam shall have the body, but not until he knows what having the body means. To instruct him further Achilleus puts before him the example of Niobe. She, like Achilleus and Priam, once thought she could achieve something on her own. She boasted that she had borne "six daughters, and six sons in the pride of their youth" (24.604; trans. Lattimore), ten more children than the goddess Leto; but the gods punished her presumption: Leto's two children immediately killed Niobe's twelve. Turned to stone, Niobe now weeps eternally, but even so, once the gods had buried her children, Niobe endured to eat. Like Niobe, Achilleus has accepted, and Priam must accept, that although the gods can and will kill everything we cherish, life can and must be embraced.

Accepting what Achilleus already has accepted—having kissed, as it were, the hands of death—Priam finds that he, too, can eat, and sleep. Gazing on each other each knows from his own experience what the other's acceptance has cost. It is easy to say, and Odysseus says it (*Il.* 19.228–33), that grief for the dead must be endured; but has anyone ever felt loss as Achilleus felt Patroklos's loss or Priam Hektor's? The greatness of Priam's and Achilleus's grief is the measure of the greatness of both the grievers and the grieved-for, and the greatest heroism of all is the grievers' acceptance of their grief.

According to Homeric ideas, the final bestower of honor is the Muse, through the agency of the poet. To the extent that we and our students can learn to feel what the Muse conveys in the *Iliad*, the glory of Achilleus is secure, in spite of, and because of, the will of Zeus.

Actively Engaging Students with Homer's Poetry

Barbara Apstein

Homer's *Odyssey* is surely one of the most appealing books ever written. It provides something for every kind of reader: the entertainment of a suspenseful adventure story complete with magical transformations, witches, and giants, as well as the illumination of many varieties of human interaction. For college students, studying the *Odyssey* can be both a pleasurable experience and a stimulus for thinking about their own world. Human nature may indeed be everywhere the same, but human institutions and systems of belief are impressively different. Many students have never examined a culture as fundamentally alien to theirs as Homer's is. As they immerse themselves in the *Odyssey*, they inevitably begin to think about their own customs and habits of mind.

I teach the *Odyssey* as part of a two-semester survey course entitled Literary Classics of Western Civilization. The first semester covers ancient through medieval times; the second, the Renaissance through the modern period. My students are usually sophomores fulfilling a literature requirement. Like most of their other general education requirements, the literature course is often regarded as a bothersome chore that merely delays concentration on the "useful" subjects they came to college to study—these days, usually business management or computer science. Surveying students to find out why they registered for Literary Classics provides some sobering data: for every student who answers "I enjoyed studying mythology in high school and would like to learn more," there are three or four who respond "I have to fulfill a requirement and this course is offered at a convenient time."

This attitude should not seem too surprising at a public college whose students are often the first in their families to continue their education beyond high school. Although their parents often expect high grades in all courses, they naturally place highest value on those subjects that they think will be translated into future economic gains. The idea that reading and analyzing literature might have some intrinsic value or that college is a place for general intellectual growth is, not surprisingly, alien to them.

Another barrier, which anyone who teaches college freshmen and sophomores must contend with, is the fact of adolescence, a stage of development that is more protracted in the United States than in other countries. It does no good to bemoan the apathy and self-centeredness of college freshmen and sophomores, to regret that they do not think and behave like adults, or to point with relief to the greater maturity of upperclassmen and adult students. Eighteen- and nineteen-year-olds, as psychologists reassure us, are no more mature than they should be; teachers must remind themselves, as generations of exasperated parents have, that adolescence is a necessary and normal stage in human psychological development and that failure to experience it may result in deeper problems in later life.

The qualities typical of adolescence, narcissism and the desire to maintain control, are, of course, far removed from the intellectual openness and willingness to explore that characterize the ideal student of literature. Adolescents are unlikely to respond to material that appears to have no immediate bearing on their lives. The combination of a narrowly pragmatic view of education with adolescent self-centeredness means that, although there are always a few highly motivated students, most are likely to be frustratingly resistant to the study of literature. I believe that for such students the Homeric poems can be approached most effectively as a springboard for exploring their own lives and their own society.

To achieve this goal, it is best to keep lecturing to a minimum. Fascinated as the instructor may be by such topics as the question of multiple authorship, the process of oral composition, or the decipherment of Linear B, he or she should put these topics aside, at least at the beginning, and concentrate on encouraging the students to respond to Homer's poetry. Even the most enthralling lecture tends to confirm these students, who often lack confidence to begin with, in their suspicion that "college literature" is difficult stuff that only the instructor can really understand and that has nothing to do with their lives anyway. Once they slip into the pattern of comfortably passive note taking to which they are so well accustomed, they can become as difficult to rouse as Odysseus's sailors among the lotus eaters, and the opportunity to engage them as active participants will be lost. Thus, although it may require considerable self-restraint *not* to lecture—so much interesting information, so few class hours—the instructor must resist.

Homeric religion is one aspect of the *Odyssey* that does intrigue adolescents. For the most part, Christianity is an unexamined part of their cultural background: they remember some Bible stories and some pious maxims, but they have never really thought about the purposes religion serves in human life. Confronting a religion so fundamentally different from their own forces them to think about this.

The question of why Poseidon is hostile to Odysseus, which emerges early in book 1, leads quite naturally into a discussion of the role of the Greek gods in general. If Polyphemos had not been Poseidon's son, Odysseus would have escaped from his encounter with the Cyclops without injury. Students soon make the observation that Poseidon's private vendetta against Odysseus and Athene's favoritism both suggest that the Greek gods are just as partial and subjective as mortals. This discovery leads them to speculate that perhaps the story of Poseidon's vengeance is a way of accounting for the unusual number of difficulties Odysseus encountered during his sea journey. Given the fact that human beings crave explanations for the events of their lives, how much more satisfying to attribute Odysseus's troubles at sea to a single cause, the hostility of a god, than to a series of unrelated accidents (bad weather, stormy seas, inept navigation). This kind of analysis usually prompts speculation about the meaning of their own religion. Isn't it possible that the story of Adam and Eve evolved as a way of explaining the harsh conditions of human existence, the fact of mortality, the subordination of women? In the context of Homeric study, such questions as these can be raised without offending believers.

Athene's affection for Odysseus leads to a similar line of thinking. Odysseus is the wisest of mortals; Athene is goddess of wisdom. Perhaps Athene represents a way of explaining to a society two thousand years from the discoveries of genetics why some people are more intelligent than others.

Once this kind of discussion has begun, students are equipped to evaluate the interventions of the gods on their own. They observe that Penelope's refusal to agree to the suitors' demands is ascribed to "a plan some god put in her mind," rather than to her own ingenuity and loyalty. Even more striking is the episode in which Athene, disguised as Telemachos, goes through the town rounding up a ship and sailors for the journey to Pylos, then puts the suitors to sleep, and finally appears in the guise of Mentor to summon Telemachos, who has nothing to do but pack his suitcase. Surely none of these events requires supernatural explanation; Telemachos could have made his own traveling arrangements and the suitors could have fallen asleep in the usual way. Such episodes stimulate some thinking about Homeric psychology; the students observe that many actions that we would ascribe to individual courage, initiative, or loyalty were attributed by the Greeks to divine intervention. The instructor can develop this point by asking how we in the twentieth century account for actions that are unexpected or out of character and, by extension, how we explain human personality. Students can think of a number of theories: they cite genetic predisposition, subconscious drives, and hormone levels, as well as considering the influence of body type and of home environment on personality. Some have heard of the theory of the four humors; others suggest the idea of astrological influence. It becomes clear that even in our scientifically sophisticated age, the question of what determines personality has spawned a bewildering variety of theories and that even psychologists are far from agreement. Students discover that the gods who at first seemed so alien represent in part a primitive attempt to explain the enigma of human personality—an enigma we are still very far from unraveling. Reading Homer thus provides students with the kind of detachment social anthropologists might have in relation to their own society.

The subject of women's place in the Homeric world can evoke a lively response. Students who have read book 1 often comment on Athene's disguise. Why, they ask, does she visit Telemachos in the form of a man, Mentes, rather than a woman? Even at this early stage in their reading, students can sense that it would be unlikely for a woman, especially one of Telemachos's social class, to be traveling alone and that it would also be unlikely for a warrior like Odysseus to have a female "old friend" who might casually drop in on him in Ithaka. These ideas lead naturally into a discussion of the heroic life with its male orientation and its glorification of physical strength and courage in battle. The treatment of women is of particular interest since the feminist movement has had some impact on the thinking of nearly all the female members of the class and quite a few of the men. They are quick to observe that despite Penelope's cleverness, there is never any possibility that she will venture forth to seek her husband; her role is to wait quietly at home. So utterly passive is her role that she even sleeps through the final slaughter of the suitors. Students see that she is introduced as a type rather than an individual—the beautiful, veiled queen—and they see how ancient is the stereotype that women are highly emotional: Penelope weeps at the poet's song about the homecoming of the Achaians; Telemachos does not inform her of his departure because she would be too upset. They are surprised at how powerless she is, for a queen, as revealed by both Athene's and the suitors' assumption that Telemachos has the authority to insist that his mother remarry. It is clear that none of the suitors are in love with Penelope, that she is desirable only because the man who marries her will have some claim to the throne of Ithaka.

Students enjoy analyzing the nature of love and the meaning of marriage in ancient society. When we are finally introduced to Odysseus himself, languishing on Kalypso's isle, students invariably wonder why the hero did not try to leave earlier. If Odysseus is really so clever and if he really loved his wife, they argue, he wouldn't have stayed with Kalypso for seven years. Clearly, he was in no hurry to get home. They also ask about the nature of Odysseus's relationship with Kalypso. Was Penelope expected to remain faithful while her husband was, in their words, "messing around" with various nymphs? The answer, of course, is yes, and these questions, like so many others, can be used to explore the different meanings of "love" at different times. When Odysseus speaks to Kalypso of his "quiet" Penelope, he does not mention her beauty, her intelligence, or any passion between them. He speaks instead of his longing for home. The *philia*, or attachment, he feels for his wife is rooted in her being a part of that home. Many kinds of love are shown in the *Odyssey*: parental and filial ties, the fellowship of warriors and comrades, the devotion of servant to master. But the kind of emotion modern readers most often refer to when they use the word *love*—the passionate, exclusive relationship between a man and a woman—does not seem to exist in Homer. The idea that romantic love, which most students regard as one of the profound experiences of their lives, is as culture-bound as the food we eat and the way we cut our hair is very provocative.

Homeric political structure also arouses some curiosity. Students are surprised to find that Telemachos has not automatically become king in place of his father and are even more surprised to discover that Laertes is still alive. If the king's son does not automatically succeed to the throne, how is the succession arranged? This question cannot be answered fully until the end of the poem, when Odysseus establishes his right to rule not simply by returning but by stringing the bow and killing his challengers. But it is clear even in the early books that a weak king could not rule for long.

Students can see why a society that values warfare so highly should make physical strength and skill prime qualifications for ruling. The instructor can ask how the conditions of political life have changed since Odysseus's day, and why it is that, in general, military prowess is no longer considered a qualification for a modern head of state. No one has suggested that American presidential candidates be required to participate in a bow-stringing contest on the White House lawn. Yet although physical strength is irrelevant to the conduct of modern affairs of state, students can name a number of politicians whose success is at least partly the result of having distinguished themselves as astronauts, war heroes, basketball and football players—careers that would have earned the approval of the Homeric male. In addition, students suggest, the popularity of the lone male combatant who overcomes enormous odds through a combination of strength, skill, and valor—in such figures as the Lone Ranger, Superman, Luke Skywalker—shows how pervasive and deeply rooted our response to this stereotyped figure is.

In a survey course, then, the emphasis should be on promoting students' active participation and on using their observations and concerns as a vehicle for discussion. Many students discover that the *Odyssey*, which at first seemed difficult to read and impossibly remote from their lives, contains little that is alien to them and much that is real.

The Study Question: An Avenue
to Understanding Homer

Elizabeth A. Fisher

"If you have a question, ask it," I encouraged my twenty-five undergraduate students; "If you are wondering about something, others in the class are wondering, too," I reassured them. I met the barrage of predictable questions with my usual answers: "Yes, Classics 71: Greek Literature and Civilization, satisfies distribution requirements in humanities," and "Yes, there will be essay questions on the exams." Only after the second meeting of the course, only after my lecture on *Odyssey* 1–6, did I encounter the question that I did not predict and could not answer. It came from a shy freshman who approached me nervously after class, Fitzgerald's translation of the *Odyssey* clasped firmly on top of her notebook. "I have a question," she began. "Fine, yes," I urged, "What is it?" "Well," she hesitated, then plunged on, "Do we have to know *all* the names in the *Odyssey* for the exam?" I stared a moment in silence, stunned by the Herculean task she envisioned: Thoosa, daughter of Phorkys; Mentes, son of Ankhialos; and the son of Mermeros, Ilos, occur in the first 250 lines of the poem, but I, with my PhD in classical philology, did not "know" those names. I hastened to reassure my worried student. "No, no," I said, "you don't have to know all the names, just the important ones." She looked relieved, then puzzled. I could imagine why she was puzzled. She had no idea which names were important and which were not. Like most of my undergraduate students in Classics 71, she had no background in ancient literature. She could not foresee the subjects I would discuss in lectures, the questions I would ask in class, or the topics I would select for essay exams. Prompting her spoken question was an unspoken and more basic one: What should I look for when I read the *Odyssey*? I translated our encounter into a question for myself: How can I help such a student?

In the years since this encounter, I have gradually developed a series of study questions for students to use as they prepare their reading assignments. Since there are only a few study questions for each assignment, students can keep the questions in mind while reading. The questions guide the students' attention to topics that will be developed in class lecture and discussion; they reflect the objectives of my course and my approach to the *Odyssey*. Different course objectives and different approaches to the *Odyssey* would suggest different study questions. The device is flexible.

My basic objective in Classics 71: Greek Literature and Civilization is to explicate aspects of Greek culture and society while examining various ancient works of poetry, history, and drama. I approach the *Odyssey* both as a social and as a literary phenomenon. As a social and cultural document, the *Odyssey* provides a wealth of evidence about religion, class structure, and the oral context of poetry in Iron Age Greece; as a work of literature, the *Odyssey* offers a sophisticated plot structure and compelling characters. In each set of study questions, an identification section of twelve to fifteen proper names focuses students' attention on the plot and characters of the *Odyssey*; the remaining questions are thematic, emphasizing social, cultural, or literary aspects of the poem. My study questions for *Odyssey* 1–6 serve both as one sample of this pedagogical device and as a basis for describing how study questions fit into class discussions and lectures.

STUDY QUESTIONS

These questions are designed to help you focus on important features of your reading in preparation for class discussion. Make notes on your reading, identifying passages by book number and (approximate) line number (e.g., *Od.* 1.5).

ODYSSEY 1–6

1. Identify the following characters. What family relationships (e.g., "husband and wife") and political relationships (e.g., "king and subjects" or "allies in war") exist among these characters? Antinoös, Athene, Kalypso, Eurymachos, Helen, Hermes, Menelaos, Nausikaa, Odysseus, Orestes, Penelope, Poseidon, Proteus, Telemachos, and Zeus.

2. Which characters in question 1 are gods? How are gods different from humans in the *Odyssey*?

3. Look up the word *epithet* in a good English dictionary (e.g., *Webster's New World, The American College*). What kinds of epithets are applied to characters in *Odyssey* 1?

Class discussion of the identification items in the first question groups these characters into four categories. (1) The family of Odysseus (Odysseus, Penelope, Telemachos): here we consider how these pivotal figures are first presented in the epic and how Telemachos and Penelope prepare the audience for the eventual appearance of Odysseus. (2) The suitors (Antinoös, Eurymachos): we examine and contrast these characters as representatives of the political challenge that awaits King Odysseus on his return. (3) Friends and familiars (Helen, Menelaos, Orestes, Nausikaa): we identify the roles that these characters take in the adventures of Telemachos and of Odysseus, discussing Orestes as a figure whose experiences parallel and motivate the deeds of Telemachos. I emphasize Orestes, Helen, and Menelaos as names so familiar in the mythological tradition of the Trojan War that an ancient audience would be especially attentive to their appearance in the narrative. (4) The gods (Athene, Kalypso, Hermes, Poseidon, Proteus, Zeus): we first relate these characters to Odysseus and his adventures; we then describe the family, which includes the four Olympian gods and Helen.

At this point, class discussion yields briefly to lecture. Since some students are not familiar with Greek mythology, I describe the Homeric pantheon, taking as my departure point the divine family already established in the discussion of the study question. I expand this family to include the remaining twelve Olympian gods and some Titans—Ouranos, Ge, Kronos, and Rhea. (Out of habit and convenience, I follow Rose, but any standard mythological handbook would do as well.) The presence of Kalypso and Proteus among the identification items occasions the observation that Homer's pantheon embraces both Olympian gods and divine outsiders. Students then contribute the characteristics of these (usually) anthropomorphic gods by answering the second study question, How are gods different from humans in the *Odyssey*? Finally, I suggest that the gods described by Homer have a venerable prehistory in Greece, and I ask students to listen for parallels with Homer's gods as I briefly outline the archaeological evidence for religion in Bronze Age Greece (I base my discussion on Guthrie). The description of Kalypso's cave (*Odyssey* 5.57–74) provides a summary vignette of a Bronze Age goddess in her lush habitat.

The third study question prepares students for a lecture on oral poetic composition and Homeric formulas. The question directs students to look up a definition of *epithet* because they frequently confuse *epithet* with *epitaph*, *epitome*, or *epigram*. Once students understand that an epithet is "an adjective or other term applied to a person or thing to express an attribute, as in Alexander *the Great*" (*The American College Dictionary*), they readily locate examples of epithets in the first books of the *Odyssey*. I use the epithets that students volunteer in class discussion to illustrate several characteristics of Homeric formulas: (1) the same epithet may recur frequently in the poem (e.g., "the grey-eyed goddess Athene," Fitzgerald 1.44); (2) more than one epithet may be repeatedly applied to the same character or object (e.g., "the grey-eyed goddess Athene" and "Athene, Zeus' daughter," Fitzgerald 2.296); and (3) an epithet may be incongruous or even inappropriate (e.g., "flippered seals, brine children," Fitzgerald 4.404; and "stately Aigisthos," Lattimore 1.29). After presenting a scheme of the Homeric hexameter verse, I explain that epithets and formulas were an essential resource for the poet who composed orally and that Homer inherited a treasure trove of formulas from earlier generations of bards. (For this discussion I rely on Kirk, *Songs* 59–68.) Because the *Odyssey* is an oral composition, the poem does not always conform to modern aesthetic standards. Homer uses language that is sometimes repetitive, as well as occasionally fulsome and incongruous to modern readers, but he is not an incompetent or unimaginative poet. He is, rather, a practitioner of an art nearly lost and almost forgotten—oral poetry.

The second set of study questions (*Odyssey* 7–12) concentrates on plot structure. There are several identification items and one thematic question: Arrange the events described in books 1–12 in *chronological* order, beginning with the fall of Troy and ending with Odysseus's homecoming. The identification items direct students' attention to various important episodes in Odysseus's adventures—the adventures with the Phaiakians, the Kikonians, Teiresias, and so forth. In class, we describe the ten-year itinerary of Odysseus from Troy to Ithaka, enumerating his major stops from the first after leaving Troy (land of the Kikonians) to the last before returning to Ithaka (Phaiakia). I explain that Homer drew the story of these adventures from mythological tradition; I follow Luce 157–69, in suggesting various strands that might have contributed to the traditional Odysseus saga (e.g., Mykenean sailing instructions, Bronze and Iron Age religious accounts). We then examine how Homer uses this traditional narrative material. Since Homer has chosen to begin his narrative shortly before Odysseus's homecoming, the elapsed time of the events actually occurring in the plot of the *Odyssey* is only about forty days. The poem thus focuses tightly on Ithaka and on Odysseus himself. We first visit Ithaka and see the effects of Odysseus's twenty-year absence; we then meet Odysseus himself as he longs to return home, resumes his journey, recounts his earlier adventures, and finally arrives in Ithaka to set his kingdom in order. What could have been no more than a long string of exotic adventures becomes, in Homer's skilled hands, a plot deliberately structured to reveal the hero's character and culminate in his greatest triumph.

The final set of study questions (*Odyssey* 13–24) focuses on social institutions and class structure in the *Odyssey*. M. I. Finley is my guide for devising this set of study questions and for leading class discussion. In the questions, I ask students to describe the members and the functions of the Homeric household and also to characterize several classes of people in the *Odyssey*: slaves, townsmen, traders, nobles, and kings. Class discussion of the lower end of the social scale is invariably interesting. Distinguishing slaves from free townsmen among such identification figures as Eumaios, Iros, Melanthios, and Philoitios raises numerous provocative questions: Where do slaves come from in the *Odyssey*? Are all free townsmen materially more comfortable or more privileged than slaves? Are free men presented as superior to slaves in character or in natural abilities? Finally, class discussion of the Homeric household provides a sort of summary exercise, drawing on passages throughout the *Odyssey*. The composition of the household and its social and economic functions can be demonstrated in Odysseus's palace at

Ithaka as it is described both before and after his return. In conclusion, we return to the first reading assignment and recall the extended family living in Nestor's household at Pylos.

Study questions have proved to be a useful pedagogical device in a number of ways. For the student who is overwhelmed on encountering the *Odyssey*'s vast and alien expanses, study questions offer a foothold in familiar territory. Before students begin reading an *Odyssey* assignment, the questions introduce them to the subjects that will be discussed in class and to the proper names that they must be able to recognize and remember. Since students are often particularly intimidated by unfamiliar proper names, I pronounce the identification items aloud in class when I distribute each set of study questions. This procedure helps students to read more attentively and to follow lectures more successfully. Students who do not know the correct pronunciation of a name like Phaiakians may confuse it with a similar name like Phoenicians, or they may invent a weird and wondrous pronunciation like "Fay-kee-uns"; alternatively, they may simply skip the word as they read. Those who skip do not recognize and retain information about the Phaiakians from their reading; those who invent or confuse pronunciations fail to recognize the word when it is correctly pronounced in the lecture. Both groups benefit from the simple expedient of reading study questions aloud in class.

Study questions also help students learn to draw general conclusions from specific evidence, a process that I consider basic to the humanistic disciplines. For years I assigned short papers and essay exams with the expectation that such exercises would teach students to assemble data, analyze them, and draw conclusions from them. For years I commented repeatedly on students' failure to demonstrate this process, writing in the margins of countless essays "You have not answered the question" or "You have not collected all the evidence to support your conclusion" or, simply, "This is vague! Be specific!" Finally, I realized that students in my introductory-level humanities course need specific and frequent direction in order to develop the ability to observe literature accurately and analyze it carefully. Class discussion of the thematic study questions provides the occasion for such specific direction. In class I can elicit from students the exact meaning and the implications of a study question, and I can discuss with them how to locate passages in the reading that provide evidence for a given question. Vague responses to the question can be met with a specific challenge: "How do you know that? What situation or character illustrates your point?" By means of class discussion, I can lead students through the process of assembling evidence, analyzing it, and drawing conclusions based on it. Essay exams and short papers become an opportunity for students to demonstrate the process that they have learned with the help of the study questions.

Study questions also provide a vehicle for conveying to students several important messages that can be demonstrated by example more effectively than they can be explained. The first of these messages is that education is the active pursuit of understanding and the active cultivation of critical abilities; education is not the passive consumption of information. The second and related message is that the basic material of this course is the work of literature, not the teacher's lectures. These two messages are conveyed through class discussion of study questions. These discussions become lively interchanges in which all who have prepared the study questions may participate on equal terms; students often cite evidence and suggest interpretations that are new to their fellow students and to me. Yet another message tacitly conveyed by the study questions is a legacy from my own student days and from my mentor, Stuart G. P. Small: "Learning to read literature is a matter of learning to ask the right questions." Readers who asked the right questions have revolutionized Homeric scholarship; Schliemann asked, "Where shall I dig to find Troy?" and Milman Parry wondered, "Could Homer have been an oral poet?" There are questions as unorthodox as Parry's and Schliemann's once were, and as revealing, still waiting to be asked. Although it is not easy to learn to ask the right questions of a work of literature, study questions demonstrate to students what the *Odyssey* can reveal if its readers only ask. Perhaps the example of study questions will someday provoke a student to ask new and right questions; in the meantime, study questions have answered the plaintive cry, "Do we have to know *all* the names in the *Odyssey*?"[1]

NOTE

[1] I am grateful to Robert A. Hadley and to Ormond Seavey, my colleagues at the George Washington University, for their very helpful comments and suggestions on this essay at various stages in its composition.

Odysseus: A Matter of Identity

Robert L. Tener

The section on Homer that I discuss is included in Great Books in Translation I, offered by the English department at Kent State University. This sophomore-level course covers the classical, medieval, and Renaissance eras. Ironically, the great literary works from those periods—the *Iliad*, the *Odyssey*, the *Aeneid*, the *Divine Comedy*, and *Don Quixote*—have sometimes been labeled by students (and even some faculty fresh from graduate school) as museum pieces. To counteract that attitude, I have focused my teaching of the *Odyssey* over the past several years by asking what it offers a modern reader. For my text I have used Robert Fitzgerald's respectable translation, which has the additional virtue of being good poetry.

The fifteen-week course that includes in part the *Odyssey*, the *Aeneid*, and *Don Quixote* is organized around that initial question, whose specific answers provide direction for the class lectures and discussions. My opening comments commit the class to reengage with those great writers to understand how their imaginative insights about the nature of men and women might influence or have affected us. No extensive separate lectures on the religious, historical, and structural patterns of the works are provided. Where necessary within the discussions, such material, unobtrusively added, helps students respond to the thinking of an age whose culture is different from ours but whose people must have responded to life as we do with thought and passion.

Homer's *Odyssey*, which is studied during the first four or five weeks, forms the core of this course, and its modern appeal is the focus of topics and discussions. In the opening lecture, for example, after providing background material on gods and goddesses, oral composition, and the epic tradition, I propose questions central to the *Odyssey* and the course. What is man's identity? What is woman's? How do we learn what it means to be a man or a woman? Does our identity lie within our physical selves? Does it reside within our genes, memories, dreams, ideas, words, and actions? Does it find its bonds in our spouses, children, and parents? May it also be a part of our homes, birthplaces, country, times, and generation?

In ensuing class discussions I suggest that Odysseus's identity seems to lie not only in his strong physical frame and skill as a wrestler and archer but also in his intellectual and rational qualities. He is intelligent and cunning; he has a sense of timing and the ability to select the right word. Above all, he can control his feelings and desires. Homer takes great pains, however, to show that these virtues are only part of his hero's identity. Time after

time, Homer implies that Odysseus's identity also involves Penelope, Telemachos, Odysseus's mother and father, his servants at Ithaka, his home,
his land, his animals, his ancestors, and, most important, his belief in and
reliance on Athene. When Odysseus comes home, he comes back to these.

Relevant extensions of these questions about identity direct discussions
for each reading. For example, with the first assignment covering *Odyssey*
1–4, the students are to consider the purpose of those books, to speculate
about the effect of the scenes in the palace at Ithaka, the hospitality and
conversations associated with Nestor, and the entertainment provided Telemachos by Helen and Menelaos. Inasmuch as those scenes focus on three
heroes who, unlike Odysseus, have come home from the Trojan War—
Nestor, Menelaos, and Agamemnon—the students are asked to reflect on
what a homecoming and a home mean. In what way are both related to
Odysseus's identity? (For an exciting book that offers insights into the nature
of home and its reflection of identity, the students are referred to Gaston
Bachelard's *Poetics of Space*.)

Because homecoming, home, and identity are intimately related, the early
discussions center on the kinds of family life and surroundings that Homer
provides. The students are asked to compare and contrast the wives (Penelope, Klytaimestra, and Helen), the husbands (Odysseus, Agamemnon,
and Menelaos), the sons (Telemachos and Orestes), and the kinds of homecoming that Menelaos and Agamemnon experienced.

For a warrior on the battlefield homecoming means the act of coming
home to a particular woman and the set of attitudes both have toward that
event. With this in mind, I raise another group of related questions for the
next two sets of readings, books 5–8 and 9–12. What is the purpose of the
scenes involving Nausikaa and those of Odysseus's adventures? What qualities are admired in a man? What in a woman? What parallels or contrasts
are there between Penelope and Nausikaa? What are Odysseus's desires?
Why is so much time spent on the adventure with Polyphemos? Why are
so many of the monsters that Odysseus encounters females? In what way
does the creation of or belief in such creatures as the Sirens and Skylla reflect
the ancient Greek male view of women? (For further ideas about these topics,
the students are referred to my article "A Portfolio for Nausicaa.")

In the discussion that develops from these questions, the students are
reminded that personal identity is as important to Odysseus as it is to us
today in an age of crises when we wonder who we are or where we are
going. Essential aspects of his identity are revealed when he shouts back to
Polyphemos, ". . . tell him / Odysseus, raider of cities, took your eye: /
Laertes' son. . ." (9.503–05). By his own words Odysseus reminds us that
identity resides not only in the present but also in the past and in the future.
What we are depends on where we came from, our ancestors and our country;

it depends on what we do in the present, often an extension of our past; and it depends on the future and what it will say or write about a man or woman. Throughout its extensions in time, identity is associated with reputation, fame, praise, and gossip. Through that relationship one's identity becomes a reflection of one's culture and language and the interaction with those. It reflects a deeply felt need in people to know their past, their birthplace, their ancestors, and their historical origins and to share that knowledge with others. We are our past. If we are to become our future, we must hold on to our past or continuously reconstruct it.

In examining this idea and applying it to Odysseus, students learn that one of the more important aspects of identity for the heroic warrior is the past, his former relationships with family, home, and land. His journey home becomes in one sense a return to his past. But the problem that the students must cope with is how Homer anchors Odysseus to his past. In what follows, they need to remember that when we first meet Odysseus he is a captive on Kalypso's island. Within a cluster of images describing Kalypso's dwelling place, Homer places Odysseus longing for his own home as he stares out at the gray sea. Homer has already been working on one of his major themes, *nostos*, or homecoming, an interesting and worthwhile discussion of which can be found in Gregory Nagy's *Best of the Achaeans*. On the island isolated from the world by the great sea, Odysseus is a nobody. If he is to restore his greatness, the essence of what makes him heroic, he must return home, to those sources that can replenish what he may have lost. In the ensuing discussions with the students, I point out that the bond between identity and homecoming is a major theme today. Like Odysseus, we are sometimes possessed by that which helped make us what we are as well as by that which can help us continue being what we are.

Although the pattern of Odysseus's quest seems resident within us, it is necessary to remind students that the *nostos* theme does not answer all our questions about the hero's identity. The epic raises other problems that are related to homecoming. For instance, why does Odysseus shout out his name and ancestry to Polyphemos? Why does he identify himself at Alkinoos's court? Why does the bard Demodokos sing the song about the wooden horse? Why is Phemios, the bard for the suitors, spared in the great battle? If we grant the need to reassert our identities and the value of the return-home pattern in our lives as seen in Odysseus, then we might go one step further and consider how identity is related to the present and the future.

In examining that bond which seems to tie us to tomorrow, we begin with the obvious. Human beings are gregarious and need to realize that other people know and talk about them. Indeed, most of us probably do not want to be forgotten; important and powerful people may feel a need to leave their signatures behind. Great figures like the artist Milton, General Patton, or Emperor Napoleon may even have a powerful or compulsive sense of historicity. Is Odysseus so different from them in that desire? He identifies himself as a "raider of cities" (9.504). Bards sing about his great deeds; Helen talks about the wooden horse, his cunning product. Today we read about him. Apparently identity as *nostos*, or return, cannot be separated from identity as *kleos*, that is, poetic fame (Nagy).

In the discussions that focus on this second theme, I try to incorporate the idea that identity for the future lies in what the future will say about one. Our TV, radio, newspapers, and biographies record our doings today, but for Odysseus there was only the bard. For future generations to know one's greatness, one had to rely on the skill of the poet who had the words and the power to retell one's achievements. That is why, I banter lightly, our world today is made of paper, literature, biographies, and movies about famous people. Our *kleos* is provided by our media. Surely our identity, as far as the future is concerned, lies in the accumulation of the written or taped record of our words and actions. As we grow older, perhaps what others say or think about us will seem even more important.

Because what the future will acknowledge about us is largely shaped by our present behavior, I ask students to analyze the relationship between identity and the physical, intellectual, and emotional surroundings. Specifically they are to determine how Odysseus relates to his environment by examining the events that the hero narrates at the court of the Phaiakians. What aspects of this relationship does Homer describe? Are there internal as well as external threats to Odysseus's identity? How does the great warrior respond to the dangers and conditions his mind or heart determines for him? What are they? Whether they are real or not for us seems beside the point; what is important is that Odysseus accepts them as real. Why does Homer provide information about Odysseus's relationship with Kalypso, Circe, Nausikaa? Why tell us the tale of Ares and Aphrodite? Last, I ask the students to consider the fact that Odysseus left Penelope when she was a young woman. He has been gone for almost twenty years. Under those conditions what have Odysseus and Penelope lost? Could that loss be a threat to his identity?

One hopes the students understand that in the quest for identity the mind can construct its own dangers: the Polyphemos, Skyllas, Sirens, and Circes of its mental uncharted oceans; it may even believe that such creatures are real. For Odysseus, they are real. But the mind can also resent losing the chance to share youth with the woman it loves. As Luigi Pirandello showed in his play *Henry IV*, a man can resist the turn of time by wanting to start life over again with a younger reflection of his older wife. Can a woman? Homer is writing about males for a male audience. And many a man dreams of eternal youth and sex. Does Homer present those visions as temptations of the mind, externalized, that can threaten Odysseus's identity?

All that can possibly prevent Odysseus's homecoming and frustrate his need for poetic fame can be seen as challenges to his identity, as much for Odysseus as they are for us. But Homer allows his hero a faith that sustains him despite the temptations from his environment. When Odysseus needs her, his patron goddess Athene is always there. Her actions and their consequences, which Homer integrates into the structure of his epic, bear on Odysseus's identity. Central to the Nausikaa episode, she is his powerful ally in the great battle against the suitors.

In our quest for identity we, like Odysseus, must survive the external and internal dangers that we encounter. The students need only recall the obvious physical dangers of our environment such as wars, pollution, hydrogen bombs, cars, and accidents. There are also spiritual and emotional threats like our confusions in belief, in loyalty, in professions, in ambition. There are even the destructive effects of our psyches such as erotic fantasies and needs, cravings for drugs, hunger for approval or power, obsessions with causes or consumerism. By these dangers we are tested just as Odysseus was. And like Odysseus, we need a sustaining faith so that through surviving and through believing, we continually reestablish our identities.

The last twelve books are assigned to be read as a unit. Since they concern the most important aspects of *nostos* and *kleos*, these books are not discussed in separate sections. The new questions on identity derive from the unity of these two themes in this portion of the epic. The students are to consider why, in a work about males and for males, Homer describes so many females, both divine and mortal: those with monstrous qualities such as the Sirens or Circe; those in the catalog of dead women; those received as mistresses by the suitors; those close to Odysseus such as his mother or his faithful servant Eurykleia; and those most closely identified with him, Penelope and Athene. Further, the students are to speculate on why Homer is so careful in developing the scenes involving Penelope. What is her relationship to the other females in the epic, to the episode of the bow and arrow, and to the final battle? Why does Homer provide us with Penelope's use of the bed to test Odysseus? In what ways does Homer show that Penelope is as necessary to Odysseus as he is to her? Could Odysseus have selected a woman as his mate who was not a Penelope? Would that have been possible for him? For her? In a world dominated by a male view, is it possible that the greatest dangers—physical, emotional, and intellectual—come from those of the feminine sex, whose responses often remain a mystery to the male psyche? Do they come from the Klytaimestras men once fell in love with? I propose to my students that sometimes we select our mates out of the depths of what we are and thus our mates tend to be reflections of us. At other times we choose mates because of our desires or obsessions, and instead of being reflections our mates are extensions or antitheses of us. Within this context the students are to determine where the greatest threats to Odysseus's identity lie: in his home? in his servants? in his son? in his wife? Are such hazards more dangerous than those from the Skyllas, Circes, and Nausikaas of life? Is Odysseus's problem when he reaches Ithaka that of Hamlet at the court of his uncle Claudius or that of our psyches when we marry?

In responding to such questions, the students are to remember that Athene is Odysseus's patron goddess. Not only is she the deity of wisdom and rational martial arts, but she is also the goddess of the domestic art of weaving, a craft that requires a readiness of hand and eye allied with proper judgment. Homer thus skillfully creates the sense that Odysseus is a rational man who has the wisdom and ready wit coupled with judgment of hand and eye to weave his way through the fabric of life and to survive. Another way to put this is that Odysseus always brings to a situation the right virtues that will enable him to survive and to win. But those virtues are identified with his patron goddess and his belief in her. It is worthwhile for the students to understand that, although the ancient Greeks conceived Athene as a female divinity, they believed that she sprang from her father Zeus's head instead of dropping from a woman's womb. In the cluster of ideas opened by this belief, Athene seems to embody that which Homer implies is the source and power of life at both the physical level—is she not invincible in war?—and the intellectual level—she contains those skills and disciplines of the mind that enable one to remain calm, rational, and in control. Apparently sexless, though clearly female, she seems to be a male form of the female. Her relationship to Odysseus, unlike that of Kalypso or Circe, is one of rational discipline.

In this context the students come to see that in the last half of the epic two major characters, Odysseus and Penelope, emerge as rational reflections of each other with separate sexual identities. Perhaps for us these have become archetypes that provide some insight into our natures and that interest us because they encompass the need to return home and gain recognition if our identities are to continue. This theme will dominate our discussions the rest of the semester. It will be important later for the students to analyze the differences between Odysseus as the archetypal rational man and Socrates as Plato's rational man. In Homer's Odysseus, identified closely with Athene, we see a rational hero whose body and mind work harmoniously together. But his ultimate goals are *nostos* and *kleos*. The first involves the restoration of harmonious living with Penelope; the second means that the world must know how the first came about. Both themes are important aspects of his identity. As a rational being, Odysseus is concerned with physical survival in an intensely dangerous environment. For his mate he chose a woman who is like him—clever, cunning, a survivor in a domestic world as threatening for her as his world away from home was for him. Her resisting the importunate and dangerous young suitors demands the same heroic fortitude that Odysseus needs to reject Nausikaa.

In discussing these topics, students come to see that there is that in modern men and women which causes us to admire, or at least to be fascinated by, cunning and cleverness. We have some respect for streetwise people who know how to survive in the ghetto. Being "streetwise," Odysseus and Penelope appeal at some level regardless of their tactics.

Though our conceptions and thoughts are formed in our native tongue, they parallel in many ways those formed by Homer despite the thousands of years between us. Our problem today is Odysseus's as it was Hamlet's. Home is where we start, where we return to, where we must decide who is loyal to us, where we gamble our lives. Homer has focused in the last half of the *Odyssey* on those dangers that develop within the home and affect our self-images. He has shown us consistently that Penelope and Odysseus take much of their sense of identity from their environment. As we approach the end of our discussions about the *Odyssey*, students learn that to explore the questing nature of men and women is to see what great artists seem to know intuitively. Identity is also important to Plato's Socrates, Vergil's Aeneas, and Cervantes's Don Quixote. These heroic figures also desire to restore harmony to their homes or countries, to rid them of evils both exploitative and destructive of everything they believe in and love. But the conception of each identity is different. If Odysseus seems to be the archetype of the rational human being who places individual physical survival over that of the group, Socrates is the rational person who places belief in the ideal, the soul, over an imperfect physical existence. Aeneas provides us with a romantic yet social archetype of someone who places duty to the state and its future over personal survival, and Don Quixote represents neither the rational nor the irrational but both simultaneously, an ironical archetype. Today Odysseus, Socrates, Aeneas, and Don Quixote are the major archetypes that influence how we determine our identity and destiny.

Teaching Homer from the Top Down:
The Telemachy

William C. Scott

Translations of the *Iliad* and the *Odyssey* are studied in a wide variety of courses including those in general and comparative literature, anthropology, religion, and philosophy. Such courses draw on the poems for their own purposes and often choose only a portion of each text for readings. The challenge, however, is to see that students come directly into contact with the whole story as Homer designed it, for only the total epic represents his thought. Yet because of their oral style, both the *Iliad* and the *Odyssey* can be easily broken apart into individual sections; as a result, it is almost too easy to omit readings in large segments of the epics, concentrating on the Achilleus story or the wanderings of Odysseus without anyone's being aware of the settings or roles of these readings within the poems. Such choices are inevitably distorting; for example, if the *Odyssey* were designed by one poet, then the concluding half of the poem, the return to Ithaka, must be more important than the first half, which should be seen as preparatory. Yet the famed wanderings of Odysseus receive major attention in courses while their subordinate role in the epic often goes largely unnoticed.

No one wants to suppress students' reading of such tales, but at the same time it is important to preserve Homer's intention in using flashback to report these tales in the more preparatory section of the poem. The same could be said about the segregated discussion of the Patrokleia or the return of Hektor's body (*Il.* 16, 24). The analysis of isolated extracts from the poems surrenders easily to impressionism or plot summary. Today's excellent translations of the *Iliad* and the *Odyssey* are not only easy and pleasurable to read but are also successful in conveying the thought of Homer. Teachers, however, must make the full text intelligible, often in relatively few class sessions. I would propose that students and teachers achieve a balanced perspective by beginning with the broadest statements about the whole *Iliad* or *Odyssey* and then working their way down to interpretations of individual sections and scenes.

As a model for this mode of presentation I use the first four books of the *Odyssey*, called the Telemachy. That these four books have attracted their own title indicates a general conception that they are detachable from the main plot; often these books are omitted from the required reading in courses. There is even specious justification for such omission in the opening lines of book 5, which seem to repeat the scene on Olympos from the opening of book 1 as a new introduction; even the language of the second scene seems a direct borrowing from books 1–4. Yet the omission of these books suppresses Homer's own introduction to his poem: life in the palace of Ithaka. In addition, the repetition of language in various parts of the epic language is a basic part of Homer's style. Ignoring books 1–4 may be effective in drawing up an assignment sheet, but such efficiency is bought at a high price.

To include these introductory books within a limited schedule, discussion must begin with the broadest possible statements about the *Odyssey*. The *epic* is about Odysseus and his journey to his island home, Ithaka; this is made clear in the proem (1.9), in the first presentation of Odysseus (1.13–15, 17, 21), in the first scene on Olympos (1.56–59, 76–77, 83–87, 93–95), in the statements of suitors and Ithakans in the assembly (bk. 2), in comments by those visited in books 3 and 4, and in the words of Hermes to Kalypso as well as the situation of Odysseus in book 5:

> . . . his eyes were never
> wiped dry of tears, and the sweet lifetime was draining out of him,
> as he wept for a way home, since the nymph was no longer pleasing
> to him. By nights he would lie beside her, of necessity,
> in the hollow caverns, against his will, by one who was willing,
> but all the days he would sit upon the rocks, at the seaside,
> breaking his heart in tears and lamentation and sorrow
> as weeping tears he looked out over the barren water.
>
> (5.151–58; trans. Lattimore)

This desire to return to his home is reinforced through the series of choices made by Odysseus to continue his journey during his wanderings (bks. 6–12); moreover, the reestablishment of his home remains his constant goal throughout the plotting once he has landed on Ithaka. The epic ends with Odysseus as husband in his house, father within his family, and king in his palace as well as throughout his realm.

This driving desire to regain his home is the motivating force throughout virtually every book of the *Odyssey*. As such, it provides the broadest statement of the theme of the epic and should therefore underlie all finer analysis, if the approach I have suggested is correct. Of special concern at the moment, it should allow books 1–4 an important place in introducing this theme. Establishing such a relationship may seem difficult because the Telemachy concerns not Odysseus's journey but the frustration and travels of his son. Only at the beginning of book 5 does the plot return directly to Odysseus. Similarly, books 2–8 of the *Iliad* present the course of the battle in the absence of the hero, a parallel that should make us curious about the role of such a technique in enhancing the themes of the epic rather than in furthering the plot.

The Telemachy focuses on the visits of Telemachos to Nestor at Pylos and to Menelaos at Sparta followed by his return to Ithaka and contrasts the life in three palaces. In book 3 Telemachos finds Nestor and his three sons on the beach offering a sacrifice to Poseidon. The ceremony is formal: the men of Pylos are drawn up in an ordered congregation and cattle are being slaughtered for a communal religious rite. There is feasting for the men, honor for the gods, and a desire on the part of all—even the new arrivals —to participate in establishing a fruitful relationship with their divinities. Nestor is surrounded by his sons on the beach and honored by them in the palace; they are busy learning the ceremonial role proper to future kings and are preparing the sacrifice under Nestor's supervision. One of these sons, Peisistratos, willingly accompanies Telemachos as he continues his journey to Sparta. In addition, the giving of friendship to a guest and the extending of every courtesy to the son of a friend and hero pervade the book. Nestor invites Telemachos and Athene/Mentor to participate in the ceremony, honors them with prize portions of meat, and gives them lodging and a ready escort for the next day.

The situation in Sparta (bk. 4) differs in details, but the degree of welcome is the same. Telemachos arrives in the midst of another ceremony—this time, the marriage of Menelaos's daughter. Appropriately there is music and entertainment; Telemachos and Peisistratos marvel at the beauty and elegance of the palace; the guest-friendship theme is emphasized in Mene- laos's remonstrance to one of his comrades, Eteoneus, who hesitates to receive the new arrivals. Once the guests are received, their horses are cared for and they are bathed, given the prize ox-chine, and officially wel- comed. The guest-friendship motif is also used to characterize the host. Menelaos is long-winded, sufficiently dull not to recognize Telemachos (even though Helen recognizes him immediately), inept in mentioning Odysseus's name and causing Telemachos to weep, and graceless in offering him a gift that Telemachos must refuse as inappropriate. Yet the fact is that guest friendship is given freely and openly by this jovial host; bumbling as he is, he is nonetheless a successful king, at home with his wife and family, and in control of a functioning and ordered kingdom.

In both palaces Telemachos finds deep love and respect for Odysseus and a hatred for the life that the suitors have inflicted on Ithaka. The mark of this affection is the ease with which men will talk about old times and recall their previous contacts with one another. For both Nestor and Menelaos the golden years have arrived, and there is great delight to be found in reliving their earlier ventures. But there is also a desire for the correct telling of true stories about the outside world. Such storytelling is an oral society's means of keeping up with events and transmitting the best values of their culture. The tales of heroism and adventure are told with willingness and zeal; they provide pleasure for the old and instructive models of behavior for the young. Telemachos finds his most prominent model in Orestes, but he also hears the exploits of others and comes to learn firsthand of the love and admiration for his father.

Framing these two visits is the palace and broader community of Ithaka. The situation inside the palace is the subject of book 1; the condition of the community is the focus of book 2. At the end of book 4, when the suitors learn that Telemachos has disappeared, they plan to ambush him. Penelope learns of their plot, laments her plight, and drifts off to sleep in sorrow both for herself and her missing husband. There have been several studies (most prominently by van Otterlo and Whitman) that have shown the importance of ring composition as a framing device in structuring oral narrative. The Telemachy is a small but carefully designed unit, framed by ring composition, offering a contrast between life in the palace on Ithaka and the two palaces of Nestor and Menelaos. This contrast is not given in analytical style, but the terms of the contrast are as carefully balanced as they could be in a narrative mode. Nestor appears surrounded by his obedient sons, who are preparing to take over the kingship; Telemachos is a son without a father and without a kingship since there seems no acceptable rule of succession while the suitors dominate his palace. The assembly is unable to take any action in the face of the suitors' threats. The suitors have a stake in blunting all efforts at leadership, and it is only by deception that Telemachos can leave Ithaka to inquire about his father's fate. In both Pylos and Sparta, cattle are being slaughtered and banquets being held to celebrate important occasions. In Ithaka, cattle are slaughtered daily; there are no special occasions. Life moves ahead with one day indistinguishable from the last as the suitors wait for the decision that Penelope refuses to make. The banquet in Ithaka is a never-ending one where the guests were never invited, never go home, and devour someone else's food and wealth against his wishes. Nestor leads his community in prayers to Poseidon; in Ithaka clear omens, like that of the two fighting eagles in book 2, are simply dismissed by the suitors. They have no real desire to acknowledge divine messages that might be threatening. Strangers are greeted with indifference or suspicion in Ithaka; Athene/Mentes must wait to be welcomed on her arrival at the palace, and Telemachos must tell the suitors lies about the true identity of his visitor. Music is used to celebrate the marriage of Menelaos's daughter; besides the fact that no marriage is being celebrated in Ithaka—neither Penelope's nor Telemachos's—what music there is covers the conversation of Telemachos and Athene so that they can talk freely to each other during the meal with the suitors. By contrast, free conversation about old times and current news does not have to be hidden during social occasions in the other two places.

This is just a partial listing of the contrasts that can be found between the palaces of Nestor and Menelaos, on the one hand, and the palace at Ithaka, on the other. It is clear that the two older kings are living in palaces where life is organized, productive, and meaningful; where men welcome divine intervention and where they do not flee true stories from the outside world. Ithaka, conversely, offers a life that is chaotic, withering to initiative, and paralyzed. The mainland palaces are described as realms in which the individual, the family, and the community are enhanced. In contrast, the palace at Ithaka is filled with inversions of normal life: the master becomes the slave, the guests become masters, a young man cannot grow, the party never ends and the guests will not go home, the house is being destroyed by the guests, the majority of the community is terrified by the minority, and every action is done by stealth and covered by lies in the hope that no one will discover it.

How is this intricately designed and tightly framed unit meant to serve as an introduction to the *Odyssey*'s major theme, the return of the hero Odysseus to his home? By placing at the very beginning of his epic this contrast between the quality of life possible in various palaces, Homer is consciously raising his creation from the level of an adventure story to that of an epic, a work with broader ethical and social implications. The main character of the adventure story is Odysseus, and he is appropriately featured in the proem. But this epic is meant to teach lessons, creating in Odysseus an ethical model that all men should wish to follow. Homer emphasizes this ethical purpose by making it control the introduction to his poem, extending it to a length of four books, and underlining it by use of contrast. He first tells of life in the palace that is not a home, because the king—the center of the community—has been displaced; he then reinforces this description of an anti-home by showing two palaces where normal life flourishes because a king is present and dominant. Only in book 5 does he begin his epic again, turning to Odysseus, whose strong desire is not so much to leave Kalypso as it is to return to his home. At this point Homer's audience will have learned what Odysseus means by the word "home." Odysseus intends not only to return to the palace where there is a void in his family and his community but also to reinstate himself as king so that his palace will offer the full rewards of human existence portrayed in the palaces of Nestor and Menelaos. Home—as Odysseus, his family, and his friends remember it— will be restored only when he has rid his kingdom of the pervasive doubt, cynicism, and purposelessness of the suitors.

This essay is based on the premise that there are two major ways to teach the *Iliad* and the *Odyssey*—from the bottom up or from the top down. Teachers may either begin by commenting on individual scenes and books with the intent of building up to an overall statement of the meaning of the epic, or they may begin with major statements and work down to the individual scene. If time were no object, then the first would clearly be preferred since it offers stronger possibilities for study and criticism. But since time is so often a problem in treating such large and varied poems as the Homeric epics in courses in translation, I suggest that teachers consider the second method. If adequate general statements of the theme are made at first, then all the books of the epic will have a share in it; even though time for discussion of some sections will be slight, none will be omitted. If all sections of the *Iliad* and the *Odyssey* are included in this way, impressionism will not dominate and Homer's own thought will be inevitably brought into the discussion.

The Aristotelian Unity of Odysseus's Wanderings

Rick M. Newton

Anyone who has taught Homer's *Odyssey* has been faced with this question: "Can we take Homer's text as if it were a map and sail the Mediterranean, retracing Odysseus's path?" Many students with previous exposure to the *Odyssey*, perhaps from a course in mythology or literature, recall hearing that the Cyclops's cave can be found in southern Italy or Sicily and that the lotus eaters lived near Africa. They may have seen the CBS film *The Search for Ulysses*, based on Ernle Bradford's *Ulysses Found*, or they may have traced the hero's travels on a map of the ancient world. The fascinating question of the historicity of the adventures has intrigued Homer's readers from antiquity to the present. The instructor may find this issue a good springboard to stimulate students' thinking. When the question arises in class, there arises simultaneously an opportunity to address some important questions about literature and its relation to the "real world." For the larger question at issue is the difference between fiction and actuality, or, to use Aristotle's terms, between poetry and history. In considering this question, students are compelled to examine the way they interpret a work of literature. This essay suggests an approach to the discussion of this question. Our guide will be the fourth-century philosopher Aristotle, whose *Poetics* offers many insights into Homer's poetic achievement.

According to Aristotle, poetry and history differ in scope. History provides an account of specific events that do happen. But poetry has a wider range and depicts the sorts of things that can happen. Aristotle draws this distinction in the *Poetics*:

> It is not the function of the poet to relate what has happened but what can happen according to the law of probability or necessity. Whether the writer is a historian or a poet is not to be determined by whether he uses metre or prose; for the writings of Herodotus could be put into metre and still be history just as completely with metre as without it. The difference between a poet and a historian is this: the historian relates what has happened, the poet what could happen. Therefore, poetry is something more philosophic and of more serious import than history; for poetry tends to deal with the general, while history is concerned with delimited particular facts. An instance of "the general" . . . is this: what are the sorts of things which . . . various types of individuals tend to do and say? This is what poetry aims to make evident when it attaches names to characters. (1451A36–B10)

Aristotle's comments here reinforce his insistence elsewhere in the treatise that poetry's essence lies in its "imitation of the serious and noble." If Homer is a poet who fits this definition, we should be able to detect a serious and philosophic plan in the arrangement of Odysseus's adventures.

If we may speak of a traditional arrangement of adventures that have their origins in history, there are indications that Homer departs from this scheme. In the account that Odysseus gives to the Phaiakians, the Cyclops episode comes quite early: it is the third adventure the hero relates and the first to receive a protracted account. It is probable, however, that in a historically based scheme, the Cyclops episode came near the end of the wanderings, for this adventure involves only one of Odysseus's ships. Having led his fleet of twelve into the harbor of the neighboring island, Odysseus departs the next day for Polyphemos's island, taking one ship. After the encounter with the monster, he rejoins his fleet. He goes literally out of his way to see the Cyclops. The suggestion presents itself, therefore, that in the pre-Homeric arrangement this episode occurred after Odysseus had lost his other ships, that is, after the Laistrygonian encounter. If this suggestion is correct, Homer relocates the episode in an arrangement of his own. We find another indication of rearranged episodes in the Circe-Hades-Circe sequence in books 10–12. Mythological tradition associates Circe, the daughter of the Sun, with the East. She is the aunt, for example, of Medea, who comes from Kolchis. In *Odyssey* 12.4 (Rieu) Homer refers to Aiaia as "the island of the rising sun." The entrance to the underworld, on the other hand, is traditionally associated with the West, the land of the setting sun. On his way to Hades, Odysseus passes the land of the Kimmerians, "the city of perpetual mist . . . where dreadful night has spread her mantle over . . . that unhappy folk" (11.15–19). But Homer does not mention the number of days required to travel from Aiaia to the entrance to Hades. The impression is that the ship fairly flies. But if these two locations are so geographically distant from each other, the suggestion again presents itself that Homer is rearranging the traditional sequence. If he is doing so, he is replacing "history" with "poetry."

A cursory glance at books 9–12 reveals that Homer follows a simple scheme. Aside from book 11, which deals solely with the underworld, the other three books each present three adventures. In book 9 (triad I) Odysseus meets the Kikonians, the lotus eaters, and the Cyclops. In book 10 (triad II) he visits Aiolos, the Laistrygones, and Circe. In book 12 (triad III) he encounters Skylla and Charybdis, the Sirens, and the sacred cattle of Thrinakia. Within each book the first two adventures are narrated briefly, the third receiving a protracted account. The single adventure in the eleventh book also reveals a tripartite division. In the first section (lines 1–332) Odysseus tells of his approach to Hades and his meetings with Teiresias, his mother, and the noblewomen of the past. The narrative is suddenly interrupted when Odysseus asks the Phaiakians if they would like to retire for the night. This interruption forms the second section. In the third section (lines 385–630)

Odysseus resumes his narration, telling of the heroes he met in the under-world.

Uniting the diverse episodes in these four books is a series of repeated themes and motifs. One such motif is cannibalism: in triad I the Cyclops devours six of Odysseus's men; in triad II the Laistrygonians harpoon and eat the men from eleven ships; and in triad III Skylla's six heads each eat one man. Of the three adventures in each book, only one deals with can-nibalistic monsters. Of these three monster-adventures, furthermore, only one (the Cyclops episode) receives a protracted account. The other two are narrated briefly.

Before proceeding with the examination of the wanderings, let us consider another passage from the *Poetics*. The essential element in a poetic com-position, says Aristotle, is the plot, by which he means "the arrangement of events." He writes:

> Some people think a plot can be said to be a unified one if it merely centers about one person. But this is not true; for countless things happen to that one person some of which in no way constitute a unit. In just the same way there are many actions of an individual which do not constitute a single action. Therefore, those poets who write a Heracleid, a Thesiad, and poems of that kind appear to be following a wrong principle; for they think that since Heracles was a single individual any plot dealing with him must of necessity have unity. But Homer, just as he excels in other matters, seems, either through natural insight or art, to have been right in this also; for in composing an *Odyssey* he did not include an account of everything which happened to Odysseus. . . . But Homer has made both the *Iliad* and the *Odyssey* centre around an action which is unified in the sense we are demanding.   (1451A16–35)

At this point Aristotle suggests a test for poetic unity:

> The different parts of the action must be so related to each other that if any part is changed or taken away the whole will be altered and disturbed. For anything whose presence or absence makes no dis-cernible difference is no essential part of the whole.

Let us apply Aristotle's formula to the wanderings. Does Homer follow a plan of poetic unity? What is the central action that Aristotle detects? Can we remove or rearrange any of Odysseus's adventures without disturbing the whole?

It is clear that Homer conceives of the adventures in thematic terms. We see a pattern of motifs in the other thematic groups. The lotus eaters, for example, pose no physical threat to Odysseus, but they are nevertheless a dangerous obstacle in the homeward journey. For they offer the Greeks the honey-sweet fruit of the lotus, whose narcotic effects cause the men "to forget they have a home to return to" (9.97). Odysseus resorts to force in bringing the scouts back to the ship and even chains them to the benches. A similar pattern emerges in the encounter with the Sirens, whose song casts a spell of forgetfulness on "the man who draws near them unawares" (12.42). Now, however, Odysseus is bound to the ship, his hands roped to the mast. The lotus eaters in triad I and the Sirens in triad III both receive brief accounts. It is the thematically parallel Circe episode in triad II that is given a fuller narration. Circe poses no threat of physical danger. Indeed, after she restores the members of the crew to their human form, they are younger and more handsome than before. Nevertheless, Odysseus and his men deal harshly with one another. On hearing their commander organize a party to scout the island, the men "burst into sobs and tears streamed down their cheeks. But they might have spared themselves their lamentations for all the good they did" (10.201–02). After an entire year with the enchantress the men must prod Odysseus to leave. The danger posed by these adventures is the threat of relinquishing the quest, of succumbing to the temptations of drugs, women, and song; it is the threat of forgetting oneself and becoming, as it were, a pig to laziness and sensual gratification.

The Kikonians, Aiolos, and Thrinakia await discussion. This thematic group may be the most important in the poet's estimation. For he frames the entire set of adventures with episodes from it: the Kikonian episode is the first narrated adventure, the Thrinakian episode the last. Their unifying theme is identified by Zeus himself in the opening of the poem: "What a lamentable thing it is," complains the Olympian to the assembly of gods, "that men should blame the gods and regard *us* as the source of their troubles, when it is their own wickedness that brings them sufferings worse than any which Destiny allots them" (1.32–34). Zeus cites the example of Aigisthos, who defied a divine warning and murdered Agamemnon. Aigisthos paid for his crime by falling to the vengeful Orestes. In the episodes from this group the folly of Odysseus's men provides the unifying element. After the raid on the Kikonians Odysseus orders the men to return to the ships, for "there was plenty of wine, plenty of livestock" (9.45–46). But the "great fools" (*mega nêpioi*) continue eating and drinking. As a result, the Kikonians have time to summon allies and launch a counterattack. "Six warriors from each of my ships were killed," Odysseus laments (9.60–61). Disaster could have been avoided had the crew heeded its commander. The same problem lies at the root of the disaster in the Aiolos episode. With the adverse winds securely enclosed in Aiolos's bag, the fleet comes within sight of Ithaka. Odysseus falls asleep, however, and the men open the pouch, believing it to contain silver and gold. Driven back to Aiolia by the released winds, the crew have only themselves to blame: "Aiolos' measures were doomed to failure, for we came to grief, through our own criminal folly" (10.26–27). The theme is in operation again in the fully narrated Thrinakian episode. Though sternly warned not to touch the sacred cattle, the men lose their self-control when Odysseus falls asleep. The arrogant Eurylochos induces them to disobey their captain. Like Aigisthos, they are fools (*nêpioi*, 1.8) for ignoring the gods' commands.

We do not have far to seek when asking why Homer gives this group of adventures such prominence. Central to the poem is the subject of human folly, which manifests itself in uncontrolled eating and drinking. Just as Zeus raises the question of human suffering in book 1, Homer offers an answer by the end of the poem. The crew of Odysseus is analogous to the suitors in his house. The poet underlines the parallel by giving their respective leaders similar-sounding names: the spokesman for the crew is Eurylochos, the leader of the suitors Eurymachos. But most significant is that Homer assigns the two groups the identical crime and punishment. Both defy divine warnings in their violation of the sacred: the suitors, warned by omens and prophets that their demise is at hand, continue to slaughter Odysseus's livestock and desecrate his home; the crew, similarly warned, violate the sacred cattle of Hyperion. The destruction of both groups comes, then, as a punishment from the gods. Zeus is correct in his assessment of human suffering: the gods do not arbitrarily inflict sufferings on mortals; only people who are guilty of recklessness are fatally punished.

Homer fits Aristotle's definition of a poet, therefore, and also passes the Aristotelian test for poetic unity. For there is a master plan in the poet's mind that subordinates individual incidents to the larger scheme and high-lights those episodes that are thematically identical to the themes of the poem as a whole. To relocate or remove any episode from these books would indeed alter the larger pattern. Set forth in a diagram, Homer's plan of poetic unity looks like this (protracted accounts printed in capital letters):

	Adventure	Theme
	Kikonians	Folly
Triad I	Lotus Eaters	Temptation
(Book 9)	CYCLOPS	MONSTERS
	Aiolos	Folly
Triad II	Laistrygones	Monsters
(Book 10)	CIRCE	TEMPTATION
(Book 11)	HADES	DEATH
	(Hades-Phaiakia-Hades)	
	Skylla (and Charybdis)	Monsters
Triad III	Sirens	Temptation
(Book 12)	THRINAKIA	FOLLY

In this arrangement Homer provides specific examples of the three *sorts* of things that can happen to anyone in pursuit of a goal: one may encounter overwhelming and monstrous obstacles, succumb to temptation and simply give up, or commit a reckless error that results in the failure to attain the goal. This is the "serious" and "philosophic" issue addressed in the poem of the wanderings. Homer, *qua poeta*, does not relate what specifically happened to a single man as he traveled from one geographic location to another. Such details are matters for the historian, not the poet.

It is significant that Homer interrupts the thematic sequence with the account of Odysseus's visit to the underworld. This episode stands out of the pattern of adventures and holds a prominent place. Odysseus proceeds to Hades from Circe's island and then returns to Aiaia to bury Elpenor. Framed, as it were, by the death and burial of Elpenor, the journey to the underworld comes as a break in the flow of the narrative. This suddenness reflects the nature of death itself, for death is the ultimate obstacle in one's pursuit of a goal. When it comes, furthermore, it may be unanticipated. For this reason, Homer inserts a surprise interruption within the book, breaking the spell of Odysseus's tale and bringing the audience back to Phaiakia. Odysseus himself registers surprise in the underworld when he sees the spirit of his mother among the shades. The manner in which the subject of death intrudes itself into the sequence calls to mind the remarks of the chorus in the famous "Ode to Man" in Sophocles's *Antigone* (332–75). Celebrating the accomplishments of the human race, this ode could be read as a song to Odysseus, the epitome of human versatility: "Many are the wonders that walk the earth, but nothing so wondrous as man." In Sophocles's catalog of achievements, man crosses the sea with his own ships, ploughs the earth with yoked oxen, builds cities and protects himself from the elements, has taught himself language and the skills of civilization, and has even discovered cures for diseases. "He is all-inventive," the chorus continues. "He has the means to face any situation. It is from death alone that he has no escape" (trans. mine).

In arranging the adventures of the hero, then, Homer leaves out nothing significant, nor does he include anything superfluous. He presents an imitation of an action that, in Aristotelian terms, is serious, complete, and ample, and he composes this imitation using general and philosophic principles as his guide. The reader who responds to the adventures by wanting to believe that they actually occurred is responding to Homer's poetic treatment of quasi-historical subject matter. The *Odyssey* seems to speak to each reader individually. Some four hundred years after Homer, the rhetorician Alcidamas wrote, "The *Odyssey* is a fair mirror of human life." Our response to Homer today is identical to the famous reaction that Aristophanes of Byzantium, in the third century BC, registered after studying Menander: "O Homer, O Life, which one of you has imitated the other?"

PARTICIPANTS IN SURVEY OF HOMER INSTRUCTORS

The following scholars and teachers of the Homeric epics generously agreed to participate in the survey of approaches to teaching the *Iliad* and the *Odyssey* that preceded preparation of this volume. Without their assistance and support, the volume would not have been possible.

Barbara Apstein, Bridgewater State College; Kenneth J. Atchity, Occidental College; Apostolos N. Athanasakis, University of California at Santa Barbara; Norman Austin, University of Arizona; Albert R. Baca, California State University; James R. Baron, College of William and Mary; William C. Bradford, College of Charleston; Sr. M. Teresa Brady, College of White Plains of Pace University; Shelby Brown, Dartmouth College; Mitzi M. Brunsdale, Mayville State College; Sara Burroughs, Northern State College; Howard Clarke, University of California, Santa Barbara; William Clarkson, University of the South; Mary Clawsey, Cappin State College; Lawrence J. Clipper, Indiana University, South Bend; Thomas J. Corr, West Chester University; Owen Cramer, Colorado College; Paul Desjardins, Haverford College; George E. Dimock, Smith College; Marya M. DuBose, Augusta College; Margery S. Durham, University of Minnesota; George D. Economou, University of Oklahoma; J. Joel Faber, Franklin and Marshall College; Robert Fagles, Princeton University; Elizabeth A. Fisher, George Washington University; William K. Freiert, Gustavus Adolphus College; Catherine Freis, Millsaps College; Harris Friedberg, Wesleyan University; Susan R. Gannon, Pace University; Edward V. George, Texas Technical University; Edgar M. Glenn, California State University, Chico; William F. Hansen, Indiana University; Philip T. Heesen, Millersville University; Frances L. Helphinstine, Morehead State University; Gail C. Holan, Georgian Court College; Donald Keesey, San Jose State University; Cynthia King, Wright State University; David Konstan, Wesleyan University; Lawrence B. Lebin, Lock Haven University; Ronald P. Legon, University of Illinois, Chicago; Daniel B. Levine, University of Arkansas; Sally MacEwen, Agnes Scott College; Kevin J. Madden, Georgetown University; Alice S. Mandanis, Marymount College; John D. McKee, New Mexico Institute of Mining and Technology; John McLaughlin, East Stroudsberg University; Wallace McLeod, University of Toronto; Douglas J. McMillan, East Carolina University; D. Gary Miller, University of Florida; Michael N. Nagler, University of California, Berkeley; Rick M. Newton, Kent State University; Catherine C. Nicholl, Augsburg College; Susan Noakes, University of Kansas; J. Frank Papovich, University of Virginia; Harry Preble, Missouri Southern State College; Paul Properzio, Drew University; Norman Rabkin, University of California, Berkeley; Ann R. Raia, College of New Rochelle; Stella Revard, Southern Illinois University; John E. Rexine, Colgate University; Edward L. Richards, Jr., Norwich University; Clark Rodewald, Bard College; C. M. Rothrauff, State University College of New York, Potsdam; John E.

Rowland, Wake Forest University; Donald N. Schweda, Quincy College; William C. Scott, Dartmouth College; David Shusterman, Indiana University Southeast; Clyde Curry Smith, University of Wisconsin, River Falls; Joseph R. Tebben, Ohio State University; Robert L. Tener, Kent State University; G. Ray Thompson, Salisbury State College; James Tipton, Alma College; Maxine Turnage, North Texas State University; Robert W. Ulery, Jr., Wake Forest University; John Ward, West Chester University; William Whallon, Michigan State University; Eliot Youman, Mercer University; Robert Zaslavsky, Bryn Mawr Library.

WORKS CITED

Books and Articles

Aarne, Antti, and Stith Thompson. *The Types of the Folk-Tale: A Classification and Bibliography*. Trans. and enl. Stith Thompson. Helsinki: Folklore Fellows Communications 184, 1961.

Abercrombie, John. *Computer Programs for Literary Analysis*. Philadelphia: U of Pennsylvania P, 1985.

Adkins, A. W. H. "Classical Studies: Has the Past a Future?" *Didaskalos* 3 (1969): 18–35.

———. *From the Many to the One: A Study of Personality and Views of Human Nature in the Context of Ancient Greek Society, Values, and Beliefs*. Ithaca: Cornell UP, 1970.

———. *Merit and Responsibility: A Study in Greek Values*. Oxford: Oxford UP, 1960.

———. *Moral Values and Political Behaviour in Ancient Greece: From Homer to the End of the Fifth Century*. New York: Norton, 1972.

Alain [pseud]. *The Gods*. Trans. R. Pevear. New York: New Directions, 1974.

Allen, Thomas W. *Homeri Opera*. 5 vols. Oxford Classical Texts. Oxford: n.p., 1906.

Aristotle. *The Poetics of Aristotle*. Trans. Preston H. Epps. Chapel Hill: U of North Carolina P, 1970.

Arnold, Matthew. On the Study of Celtic Literature *and* On Translating Homer. New York: Macmillan, 1899.

———. *On Translating Homer*. London: n.p., 1905.

Arthur, M. "The Divided World of *Iliad* VI." *Reflections of Women in Antiquity*. Ed. Helen P. Foley. New York: Gordon, 1981. 19–43.

Atchity, Kenneth John. *Homer's* Iliad: *The Shield of Memory*. Carbondale: Southern Illinois UP, 1978.

Austin, Norman. *Archery at the Dark of the Moon: Poetic Problems in Homer's Odyssey*. Berkeley: U of California P, 1975.

———. "Odysseus and the Cyclops: Who Is Who." *Approaches to Homer*. Ed. Carl A. Rubino and Cynthia Schelmerdine. Austin: U of Texas P, 1983. 3–37.

Bachelard, Gaston. *The Poetics of Space*. Trans. Maria Jolas. Boston: Beacon, 1972.

Bandinelli, Ranuccio Bianchi. *Hellenistic-Byzantine Miniatures of the* Iliad *(Ilias Ambrosiana)*. Olten, Switz.: Urs Graf, 1955.

Benardete, Seth. "Achilles and the *Iliad*." *Hermes* 91 (1963): 1–16.

———. "The Aristeia of Diomedes and the Plot of the *Iliad*." *AGON* 1 (1968): 10–38.

Benner, Allen Rogers, ed. *Selections from Homer's* Iliad. 1903. New York: Irvington, 1976.

Benveniste, Emile. *Le vocabulaire des institutions Indo-Europennes.* 2 vols. Paris: Gallimard, 1969.

Bespaloff, Rachel. *On the* Iliad. Trans. Mary McCarthy. 1947. Princeton: Princeton UP, 1970.

Beye, Charles Rowan. *The* Iliad, *the* Odyssey, *and the Epic Tradition.* New York: Doubleday, 1966.

Bianchi, Martha Dickinson. *The Life and Letters of Emily Dickinson.* Boston: Houghton, 1924.

Bland, David. *A History of Book Illustration.* Berkeley: U of California P, 1969.

Bowra, C. M. *Ancient Greek Literature.* New York: Oxford UP, 1960.

———. *The Greek Experience.* Cleveland: World, 1957.

———. *Heroic Poetry.* London: Macmillan, 1952.

———. *Homer.* New York: Scribner's, 1972.

———. *The Oxford Book of Greek Verse.* Oxford: Clarendon, 1930.

———. *Tradition and Design in the* Iliad. Oxford: Clarendon, 1930.

Briganti, Giuliano. *Italian Mannerism.* Trans. Margaret Kunzle. Leipzig: VEB, 1962.

Bryant, William Cullen, trans. *The* Odyssey *of Homer.* New York: Houghton, 1899.

Butcher, S. H., and A. Lang, trans. *The* Odyssey *of Homer.* New York: Modern Library, 1950.

Butler, Samuel, trans. *The Odyssey.* New York: Washington Square, 1969.

Camps, W. A. *An Introduction to Homer.* Oxford: Clarendon, 1980.

Carne-Ross, D. S. "The Return of Virgil." Rev. of *Aeneid,* trans. Robert Fitzgerald. *New York Review of Books* October 1983: 3–4.

Carpenter, Rhys. *Folk Tale, Fiction, and Saga in the Homeric Epics.* 1946. Berkeley: U of California P, 1962.

Chadwick, John. *The Mycenean World.* Cambridge: Cambridge UP, 1976.

———. *The Decipherment of Linear B.* Cambridge: Cambridge UP, 1958.

Chase, Alston Hurd, and William G. Perry, Jr., trans. *Iliad.* 1950. New York: Little, 1960.

Chesterton, G. K. *The Everlasting Man.* New York: Dodd, 1925.

Clarke, Howard W. *The Art of the* Odyssey. Landmarks in Literature. Englewood Cliffs: Prentice, 1967.

———. *Homer's Readers: A Historical Introduction to the* Iliad *and the* Odyssey. Newark: U of Delaware P, 1980.

———. *Twentieth Century Interpretations of* The Odyssey. Englewood Cliffs: Prentice, 1983.

Clay, Jenny Strauss. "The Beginning of the *Odyssey.*" *American Journal of Philology* 4 (1976): 313–26.

———. *The Wrath of Athena: Gods and Men in the* Odyssey. Princeton: Princeton UP, 1983.

Combellack, F. M. "Contemporary Homeric Scholarship: Sound or Fury?" *Classical World* 49 (1955): 17–26, 29–44, 45–55.

Connelly, Kenneth. Unpublished lectures. General Literature 291, Smith Coll., Amherst, MA, 1970–80.

Cook, Albert, trans. *The Odyssey*. New York: Norton, 1967.

————, trans. *The Odyssey*. Norton Critical Edition. New York: Norton, 1967.

Cotterill, Henry Bernard, trans. *Homer's* Odyssey: *A Line-for-Line Translation in the Metre of the Original*. London: Harrap, 1911.

Cowper, William, trans. *The* Odyssey *of Homer*. New York: Dutton, 1935.

Culler, A. Dwight, ed. *Poetry and Criticism of Matthew Arnold*. Boston: Houghton, 1961.

Davenport, Guy. "Another *Odyssey*." Rev. of *The* Odyssey *of Homer*, trans. Richmond Lattimore. *Arion* 1 (1968): 135–53.

Diel, Paul. *Symbolism in Greek Mythology: Human Desire and Its Transformations*. Boulder: Shambhala, 1980.

Dimock, G. E., Jr. "The Name of Odysseus." *Hudson Review* 9 (1956): 52–70.

Dodds, E. R. *The Greeks and the Irrational*. Berkeley: U of California P, 1951.

————. "Homer." *Fifty Years of Classical Scholarship*. Ed. Maurice Plantauer. Oxford: Oxford UP, 1954. 1–17.

Dover, K. J. "The Portrayal of Moral Evaluation in Greek Poetry." *Journal of Hellenic Studies* 103 (1983): 35–48.

Eliade, Mircea. *The Sacred and the Profane*. New York: Harper, 1961.

Eliot, T. S. "What Is a Classic?" *On Poetry and Poets*. New York: Farrar, 1957. 52–74.

Epps, Preston H., trans. *The* Poetics *of Aristotle*. Chapel Hill: U of North Carolina P, 1970.

Essick, Robert, and Jennijoy La Belle, eds. *Flaxman's Illustrations to Homer*. New York: Dover, 1977.

Fagles, Robert. "Homer and Writers." Steiner and Fagles 160–72.

Fenik, Bernard C. *Homer: Tradition and Invention*. Leiden: Brill, 1978.

————. *Studies in the* Odyssey. Wiesbaden: Steiner, 1974.

————. *Typical Battle Scenes in the* Iliad: *Studies in the Narrative Techniques of Homeric Battle Scenes*. Wiesbaden: Hermes Einzelschriften, Heft 21, 1968.

Finley, John H., Jr. *Four Stages of Greek Thought*. Stanford: Stanford UP, 1966.

————. *Homer's* Odyssey. Cambridge: Harvard UP, 1978.

Finley, M. I. *The World of Odysseus*. 1954. New York: Viking, 1965.

Fitzgerald, Robert, trans. *The Iliad*. New York: Anchor-Doubleday, 1974.

————, trans. *The Odyssey*. New York: Anchor-Doubleday, 1962.

————. "Postscript to a Translation of the *Odyssey*." *The Craft and Context of Translation*. Ed. William Arrowsmith and Roger Shattuck. New York: Anchor-Doubleday, 1961. 303–51.

Flaumenhaft, Mera J. "The Undercover Hero: Odysseus from Dark to Daylight." *Interpretation: A Journal of Political Philosophy* 10.1 (1982): 9–41.

Frame, Douglas. *The Myth of Return in Early Greek Epic.* New Haven: Yale UP, 1978.

Frankel, Hermann Ferdinand. *Early Greek Poetry and Philosophy.* Trans. Moses Hadas and James Willis. Oxford: Blackwell, 1975.

Frye, Northrop. *Anatomy of Criticism.* New York: Atheneum, 1967.

Gaunt, D. M. *Surge and Thunder: Critical Readings in Homer's Odyssey.* London: Oxford UP, 1971.

Geddes, William D. *The Problem of the Homeric Poems.* London: Macmillan, 1878.

Germain, Gabriel. *Genese de l' Odyssée: Le fantastique et le sacre.* Paris: n.p., 1954.

Girard, R. *Violence and the Sacred.* Trans. Patrick Gregory. Baltimore: Johns Hopkins UP, 1977.

Glover, T. R. *The Springs of Hellas.* Cambridge: Cambridge UP, 1945.

Gordon, Cyrus. *Before the Bible: The Common Basis of Greek and Hebrew Civilization.* New York: Harper, 1963.

Gouldner, Alvin. *The Hellenic World.* New York: Harper, 1969.

Gransden, K. W. "Homer and the Epic." *The Legacy of Greece: A New Appraisal.* Oxford: Clarendon, 1981. 65–92.

Griffin, Jasper. *Homer.* New York: Hill, 1980.

———. *Homer on Life and Death.* New York: Oxford UP, 1980.

Grunchec, Philippe. *Le Grand Prix de Peinture: Les concours des Prix de Rome de 1797 à 1863.* Paris: Ecole Nationale Supérieure des Beaux-Arts, 1983.

Guthrie, W. K. C. "The Religion and Mythology of the Greeks." *History of the Middle East and the Aegean Region c. 1380–1000 B.C.* Cambridge: Cambridge UP, 1980. 851–905. Vol. 2 of *The Cambridge Ancient History.* Ed. I. E. S. Edwards, C. J. Gadd, N. G. L. Hammond, and E. Sollberger. 3rd ed.

Hadas, Moses. *Humanism: The Greek Ideal and Its Survival.* New York: Harper, 1960.

Hainsworth, John Bryan. *The Flexibility of the Homeric Formula.* Oxford: Clarendon, 1968.

Hamilton, Edith. *Mythology.* 1940. New York: NAL, 1969.

Hartigan, K. V. " 'He rose like a lion . . .': Animal Similes in Homer and Virgil." *Acta Antiqua Academiae Scientiarum Hungaricae* 21 (1973): 223–44.

Hartt, Frederick. *Giuliano Romano.* 2 vols. New Haven: Yale UP, 1980.

Havelock, Eric A. *Preface to Plato.* Cambridge: Harvard UP, 1963.

Haymes, Edward R. *A Bibliography of Studies Relating to Parry's and Lord's Oral Theory.* Cambridge: Harvard U Publications of the Milman Parry Collection, 1973.

Hegel, G. W. F. *Hegel: Texts and Commentary: Hegel's Preface to His System.* Trans. and ed. Walter Kaufmann. Garden City: Anchor-Doubleday, 1966.

Held, Julius S. *The Oil Sketches of Peter Paul Rubens*. 2 vols. Princeton: Princeton UP, 1980.

Highet, Gilbert. *The Art of Teaching*. New York: Knopf, 1950.

Hogan, James C. *A Guide to the* Iliad. Garden City: Anchor-Doubleday, 1979.

Holoka, James P. "Homeric Studies 1971–1977." *Classical World* 73 (1979): 65–150.

Horton, R. W., and V. F. Hopper. *Backgrounds of European Literature*. Englewood Cliffs: Prentice, 1975.

Housman, A. E. "The Name and Nature of Poetry." *Selected Prose*. Ed. John Carter. Cambridge: U of Cambridge, 1961. 168–95.

Hull, Denison Bingham, trans. Digenis Akritas: *The Two-Blood Border Lord*. Athens: Ohio UP, 1972.

———, trans. *Homer's* Iliad. Scottsdale: n.p., 1982.

———, trans. *Homer's* Odyssey. Athens: Ohio UP, 1978.

Jaeger, Werner. *Paideia: The Ideals of Greek Culture, I*. Trans. Gilbert Highet. Oxford: Blackwell, 1946.

Jensen, Minna Skafte. *Homeric Question and the Oral-Formulaic Theory*. Copenhagen: Museum Tusculanum, 1980.

Jones, Tom. *Paths to the Ancient Past*. New York: Free, 1967.

Kakridis, Johannes T. *Homer Revisited*. Lund: New Society of Letters, 1971.

———. *Homeric Researches*. Lund: n.p., 1949.

Kirk, G. S. *Homer and the Epic*. Cambridge: Cambridge UP, 1965.

———. *Homer and the Oral Tradition*. New York: Cambridge UP, 1976.

———. *The* Iliad: *A Commentary*. Vol. 1. Books 1–4. New York: Cambridge UP, 1985.

———. *Myth: Its Meaning and Functions in Ancient and Other Cultures*. Berkeley: U of California P, 1970.

———. *The Nature of Greek Myths*. Baltimore: Penguin, 1974.

———. *The Songs of Homer*. Cambridge: Cambridge UP, 1962.

Kossatz-Deissmann, Anneliese. *Lexicon iconographicum mythologiae classicae*. Zurich: Artemis, 1981.

Lang, A., W. Leaf, and E. Myers, trans. *The Iliad*. New York: n.p., 1930.

Lattimore, Richmond, trans. *The* Iliad *of Homer*. 1951. Chicago: U of Chicago P, 1977.

———, trans. *The* Odyssey *of Homer*. New York: Harper, 1965.

Lawrence, D. H. "Introduction to Frederick Carter's *Dragon of the Apocalypse*." *Phoenix: The Posthumous Papers of D. H. Lawrence*. Ed. E. D. MacDonald. 1936. New York: Viking, 1968. 292–303.

Lesky, Albin. *A History of Greek Literature*. Trans. James Willis and Cornelis de Heer. New York: Crowell, 1966.

Lessing, Erich. *The Adventures of Ulysses: Homer's Epic in Pictures*. Trans. Kevin Smyth. New York: Dodd, 1970.

Levin, Bernard. "My Life in Words, I: Books." *Sunday Times* 6 Nov. 1983: 33–34.

Lloyd-Jones, Hugh. *The Justice of Zeus.* Berkeley: U of California P, 1971.

Logue, C., trans. *Patrocleia of Homer. A Free Translation of Book 16 of the* Iliad. Ann Arbor: U of Michigan P, 1963.

Long, A. A. "Morals and Values in Homer." *Journal of Hellenic Studies* 90 (1970): 121–39.

Lord, Albert B. *The Singer of Tales.* Cambridge: Harvard UP, 1960.

Luce, J. V. *Homer and the Heroic Age.* New York: Harper, 1965.

MacCary, W. Thomas. *Childlike Achilles: Ontogeny and Phylogeny in the* Iliad. New York: Columbia UP, 1982.

Machinist, P. "Rest and Violence in the Poem of Erra." *Journal of the American Oriental Society* 103 (1983): 221–26.

Mack, Maynard, ed. *The Norton Anthology of World Masterpieces.* 2 vols. 4th ed. New York: Norton, 1985.

Macleod, C. W., ed. *Homer:* Iliad, *Book XXIV.* Cambridge: Cambridge UP, 1982.

Mathieu, Pierre Louis. *Gustave Moreau.* Trans. James Emmons. Boston: Little, 1976.

Mnemosyne Bibliotheca Classica Batava. Lund: Brill, 1971–80.

    Charles Segal. *The Theme of the Mutilation of the Corpse in the* Iliad. 1971.

    Anne Amory Parry. *Blameless Aegisthus: A Study of "Amymon" and other Homeric Epithets.* 1973.

    William Scott. *The Oral Nature of the Homeric Simile.* 1974.

    Richard Stoll Shannon III. *The Arms of Achilles and Homeric Compositional Technique.* 1975.

    Dorothea Wender. *The Last Scenes of the* Odyssey. 1978.

    I. M. Hohendahl-Zoetellief. *Manners in the Homeric Epic.* 1980.

Morford, M. P. D., and R. J. Lenardon. *Classical Mythology.* 2nd ed. New York: Longman, 1977.

Mueller, Martin. *The* Iliad. Unwin Critical Library. Boston: Allen, 1984.

Munro, D. B., and T. W. Allen, eds. *Homeri Opera.* 5 vols. Oxford Classical Texts. 1912–20. Oxford: Clarendon, 1957.

Murray, A. T., trans. *The Iliad.* 2 vols. Loeb Classical Library. 1924. Cambridge: Harvard UP, 1948.

———, trans. *The Odyssey.* 2 vols. Loeb Classical Library. 1919. Cambridge: Harvard UP, 1976.

Murray, Gilbert. "The *Iliad* as a Traditional Book." *The Rise of the Greek Epic.* 4th ed. 1934. New York: Oxford UP, 1960. 120–43.

Myrsiades, Kostas. "A Bibliographical Guide to Teaching the Homeric Epics in College Courses." *College Literature* 3 (1976): 237–55.

Nagler, Michael N. *Spontaneity and Tradition: A Study in the Oral Art of Homer.* Berkeley: U of California P, 1974.

Nagy, Gregory. *The Best of the Achaeans: Concepts of the Hero in Archaic Greek Poetry.* Baltimore: Johns Hopkins UP, 1979.

Nelson, Conny, ed. *Homer's* Odyssey: *A Critical Handbook.* Belmont: Wadsworth, 1969.

Nicoll, Allardyce, ed. *Chapman's Homer: The* Iliad, *the* Odyssey *and the Lesser Homerica.* Princeton: Princeton UP, 1956.

Niles, John D. Beowulf: *The Poem and Its Tradition.* Cambridge: Harvard UP, 1983.

———. "Patterning in the Wanderings of Odysseus." *Ramus* 7.1 (1978): 46–60.

Nilsson, M. P. *Homer and Mycenae.* 1933. Philadelphia: U of Pennsylvania P, 1972.

Notopoulos, J. A. "The Generic and Oral Composition." *Transactions of the American Philological Association* 81 (1950): 28–36.

Ormond, Leonee, and Richard Ormond. *Lord Leighton: Studies in British Art.* New Haven: Yale UP, 1975.

Owen, E. T. *The Story of the* Iliad. 1946. Ann Arbor: U of Michigan P, 1966.

Packard, David W., and Tania Meyers. *A Bibliography of Homeric Scholarship: Preliminary Edition 1930–1970.* Malibu: Undena, 1974.

Page, Denys. *Folktales in Homer's* Odyssey. Cambridge: Harvard UP, 1973.

———. *History and the Homeric* Iliad. Berkeley: U of California P, 1959.

———. *The Homeric* Odyssey. Oxford: Clarendon, 1955.

Palmer, George Herbert, trans. *The* Odyssey *of Homer.* New York: Bantam, 1962.

Parry, Milman. *The Making of Homeric Verse: The Collected Papers of Milman Parry.* Ed. Adam Parry. Oxford: Oxford UP, 1971.

Pirandello, Luigi. *Henry IV. Naked Masks.* Ed. Eric Bentley. New York: Dutton, 1952.

Pope, Alexander, trans. *The* Iliad *of Homer.* Ed. Reuben A. Brower and William H. Bond. New York: Macmillan, 1965.

Porphyrius. *Porphyrii quaestionum Homericarum ad* Iliadem *pertinentium reliquias.* Ed. Hermann Schrader. Leipzig: Teubner, 1880.

Raine, Kathleen. *Blake and Tradition.* 2 vols. Bollingen Series 35. Princeton: Princeton UP, 1968.

Redfield, James M. *Nature and Culture in the* Iliad: *The Tragedy of Hector.* Chicago: U of Chicago P, 1975.

Rees, Ennis, trans. *The* Iliad *of Homer.* Indianapolis: Bobbs, 1963.

———, trans. *The* Odyssey *of Homer.* New York: Random, 1960.

Rexine, John E. *The Hellenic Spirit: Byzantine and Post-Byzantine.* Belmont: Inst. for Byzantine and Modern Greek Studies, 1981.

———. "Homer and the Eternity of Man: *Iliad* 6.144–149." *Classical Bulletin* 54 (1958): 25–27.

———. "The Nature and Meaning of Justice in Homer." *Classical Bulletin* 54 (1977): 1–6.

Rieu, E. V., trans. *Iliad*. Baltimore: Penguin, 1950.

——, trans. *The Odyssey*. Baltimore: Penguin, 1946.

Rose, H. J. *A Handbook of Greek Mythology, Including Its Extension to Rome*. 6th ed. 1953. New York: Dutton, 1959.

Rosenblum, Robert. *Transformations in Late Eighteenth Century Art*. Princeton: Princeton UP, 1968.

Rosner, Judith A. "The Speech of Phoenix: *Iliad* 9.434–605." *Phoenix* 30 (1976): 314–27.

Rouse, W. H. D., trans. *Iliad*. 1938. London: Nelson, 1960.

——, trans. *The* Odyssey: *The Story of Odysseus*. New York: NAL. 1962.

Rubin, N. F., and W. M. Sale. "Meleager and Odysseus: A Structural and Cultural Study of the Greek Hunting-Maturation Myth." *Arethusa* 16.1 (1983): 137–71.

Rubino, Carl A., and Cynthia W. Shelmerdine, eds. *Approaches to Homer*. Austin: U of Texas P, 1983.

Schefold, Karl. *Myth and Legend in Early Greek Art*. Trans. Audrey Hicks. New York: Abrams, 1966.

Schein, Seth L. *The Mortal Hero*. Berkeley: U of California P, 1984.

Scherer, Margaret R. *The Legends of Troy in Art and Literature*. New York: Phaidon, 1963.

Segal, Charles, ed. *The Heroic Paradox: Essays on Homer, Sophocles, and Aristophanes*. Ithaca: Cornell UP, 1982.

Seittelman, Elizabeth. "1981: Survey of Audio-Visual Materials in the Classics." *Classical World* 74 (1981): 255–97.

——. "1984: Supplementary Survey of Audio-Visual Materials in the Classics." *Classical World* 77 (1984): 231–45.

Shaw, T. E., trans. *Odyssey*. New York: Oxford UP, 1935.

Sheppard, J. T. *The Pattern of the* Iliad. New York: Haskell, 1966.

Shewring, Walter, trans. *The Odyssey*. Oxford: Oxford UP, 1980.

Snell, Bruno. *The Discovery of the Mind: The Greek Origins of European Thought*. Trans. T. G. Rosenmeyer. Cambridge: Harvard UP, 1953.

Soleri, Paolo. *The Omega Seed: An Eschatological Hypothesis*. Garden City: Anchor-Doubleday, 1981.

Stanford, W. B., ed. *Odyssey*. 2 vols. 1947. London: Macmillan, 1981.

——. *The Ulysses Theme: A Study in the Adaptability of a Traditional Hero*. 1954. Oxford: Blackwell, 1963.

Stanford, W. B., and J. V. Luce. *The Quest for Ulysses*. New York: Praeger, 1974.

Steiner, George, and Robert Fagles, eds. *Homer: A Collection of Critical Essays*. Twentieth Century Views. Englewood Cliffs: Prentice, 1962.

Taylor, Charles H., Jr., ed. *Essays on the* Odyssey: *Selected Modern Criticism*. Bloomington: Indiana UP, 1963.

Tejera, Victorino. *Modes of Greek Thought*. New York: Appleton, 1971.

Tener, Robert L. "A Portfolio for Nausicaa." *Classical Bulletin* 49 (1973): 53–57.

Thompson, Stith. *Motif Index of Folk Literature: A Classification of Narrative Elements in Folktales, Ballads, Myths, Fables, Mediaeval Romances, Exempla, Fabliaux, Jest-Books, and Local Legends.* 6 vols. Rev. and enl. Bloomington: Indiana UP, 1955–58.

Thomson, George. *Studies in Ancient Greek Society.* 1949. New York: Citadel, 1965.

Thornton, Agathe. *People and Themes in Homer's* Odyssey. London: Methuen, 1970.

Tomory, Peter. *The Life and Art of Henry Fuseli.* New York: Praeger, 1972.

Trypanis, C. A. *The Homeric Epics.* Trans. William Phelps. Warminster, Eng.: Aris, 1977.

van Otterlo, W. A. A. *De ringcompositie als opbouwprincipe in de epische gedichten van Homerus.* Amsterdam: Noords Hollandsche, 1948.

Vidal-Naquet, Pierre. "The Black Hunter and the Origin of the Athenian Ephebeia." *Myth, Religion, and Society.* Ed. R. L. Gordon. Cambridge: Cambridge UP, 1982. 147–62.

Vivante, Paolo. *The Epithets in Homer: A Study in Poetic Values.* New Haven: Yale UP, 1982.

———. *Homer.* New Haven: Yale UP, 1985.

Wace, Alan J. B., and Frank H. Stubbings. *A Companion to Homer.* New York: Macmillan, 1962.

Walsh, Dorothy. *Literature and Knowledge.* Middletown: Wesleyan UP, 1969.

Webster, T. B. L. *From Mycenae to Homer.* 1958. New York: Norton, 1964.

Weil, Simone. *The* Iliad: *Or, The Poem of Force.* Trans. Mary McCarthy. Wallingford: Pendle Hill, 1956.

Whitman, Cedric H. *Homer and the Heroic Tradition.* Cambridge: Harvard UP, 1958.

Wiebenson, Dora. "Subjects from Homer's *Iliad* in Neoclassical Art." *Art Bulletin* 46 (1964): 23–37.

Willcock, Malcolm M. *A Commentary on Homer's* Iliad, *Books I–VI.* London: Macmillan, 1970.

———. *A Companion to the* Iliad. Chicago: U of Chicago P, 1976.

———. "Mythological Paradeigma in the *Iliad.*" *Classical Quarterly* 14 (1964): 141–54.

Woodhouse, W. J. *The Composition of Homer's* Odyssey. 1930. Oxford: Clarendon, 1969.

Woolf, Virginia. "On Not Knowing Greek." *The Common Reader.* 1925. New York: Harcourt, 1953. 24–39.

Worsley, Philip Stanhoe, trans. *The* Odyssey *of Homer.* London: Blackwood, 1861.

Wright, John. *Essays on the* Iliad: *Selected Modern Criticism.* Bloomington: Indiana UP, 1978.

Zerner, Henri. *The School of Fontainebleau: Etchings and Engravings.* Trans. Stanley Baron. New York: Abrams, 1969.

Recordings and Readings

Dyer-Bennet, Richard. *Homer's* Odyssey. Trans. Robert Fitzgerald. Dramatic readings. ICM Artists (40 W. 57 St., New York, NY 10019).

Fowle, Frank F., III. *The* Iliad *of Homer.* 5 50-min. dramatic performances. Bard Productions (7558 Byron Pl., St. Louis, MO 63105).

National Radio Theatre of Chicago. *The* Odyssey *of Homer.* Eight cassettes (600 N. McClurg Court, Suite 502a, Chicago, IL 60611).

Notopoulos, James A. *Modern Greek Heroic Oral Poetry.* Folkway Records (117 W. 46 St., New York, NY 10036). 1952–53.

Page, Denys. *The Origins of Troy, The Oral Legacy, The Seventh City, Forgotten Culture,* and *The Other Dark Ages.* Five cassettes. Pacifica Tape Library (5316 Venice Blvd., Los Angeles, CA 90019).

Films, Filmstrips, and Slides

Bertolini, Francesco, and Adolfo Padovin, dirs. *L'Odissea.* Museum of Modern Art, Dept. of Film (11 W. 53 St., New York, NY 10019). 1911.

Bradford, Ernle, writer and narr. *Search for Ulysses.* 2 pts. Carousel Films, 1966.

Cacoyiannis, Michael, dir. *Iphigenia.* Cinema 5 (595 Madison Ave., New York, NY 10022). 1977.

Camerini, Mario, dir. *Ulysses.* Audio-Brandon Films (34 MacQueston Parkway So., Mount Vernon, NY 10550). 1955.

Greek Mythology. 100 slides. Dayton Press (3235 Dayton Ave., Lorain, OH 44055).

The Greek Myths. 2 films. Encyclopedia Britannica. 1971.

Homer's Mythology: Tracing a Tradition. Film strips in 3 pts. Guidance Associates (Communications Park, Box 3000, Mount Kisco, NY 10549). 1977.

A Singer of Tales in Gary, Indiana. Film. Folklore Institute, Indiana Univ.

Structure of the Epic: The Odyssey. *Epic and Narrative.* Film in 3 pts. Narrated by Gilbert Highet. Encyclopedia Britannica. 1965.

The Voyage of Odysseus. Film. Centron Films (1621 W. 9 St., Box 687, Lawrence, KS 66044). 1982.

INDEX

155